The Organ and Choir
in Protestant Worship

THE ORGAN
AND CHOIR
IN
PROTESTANT WORSHIP

by **EDWIN LIEMOHN**

FORTRESS PRESS   PHILADELPHIA

© 1968 by FORTRESS PRESS

Library of Congress Catalog Card Number 68-15862

5706K67   *Printed in U.S.A.*   1-961

Acknowledgments

The many facets of church music forming the basis of this volume could be presented only with the cooperation and assistance of a number of persons. Librarians, both here and abroad, cooperated generously in making available the desired sources. I am particularly indebted to the following church musicians for information pertaining to the present state of church music in their respective countries:

Dr. Markus Jenny	Zürich, Switzerland
Dekan Friedrich Hofmann	Nürnberg, Germany
Cantor Willem Mudde	Utrecht, Holland
Cantor Helvig Larsen	Roskilde, Denmark
Thorleif Aamodt	Bergen, Norway
Dr. Hartwig Otte	Helmstedt, Germany
Prof. Arthur Hill (*for Finland*)	Suomi College, Hancock, Mich.
Musikdirektor Gunnar Holm	Norrkoping, Sweden
Rev. Páll Halldórsson	Reykjavik, Iceland
Redaktor Sten Carlsson	Uppsala, Sweden
Cantor Eberhard Popp	Detmold, Germany
Commander A. H. West-Byng, RN	Croydon, Surrey, England

I gratefully acknowledge also the financial support granted by the Lutheran Brotherhood Insurance Company in connection with a five-month period spent in research in Europe in 1961.

Of particular importance have been the permissions received from numerous publishers to include quotations from their publications.

Edwin Liemohn
Waverly, Iowa

Table of Contents

I

Pre-Reformation Church Music

THE USE OF INSTRUMENTAL MUSIC
EARLY PRACTICES

A brief survey of the nature and practice of church music as it existed in the period immediately preceding the fragmentation caused by the Reformation will afford a perspective enabling us to discern with some degree of accuracy the directions and dynamics of the new era.

Music has always had a prominent place in worship. The Old Testament is replete with accounts of its use by large groups of singers and instrumentalists in the Temple services. Music played a less prominent role in worship in the early Christian era. It was not until the persecutions ceased, permitting public houses of worship to be built, that a systematic plan for music in Christian worship began to evolve.

While Genesis 4:21 tells us that Jubal "was the father of all such as handle the harp and organ" and although the Old Testament refers now and then to trumpets, psalteries, and other instruments, it must be kept in mind that both instruments and music were of a most primitive type up through about the tenth century of the Christian era. Our staff system of musical notation, for example, had its beginnings in the tenth century. It is approximately in this period also that a multilinear or polyphonic music, consisting of the concurrent association of two or more melodic lines, replaced the simple chant.

Music has always been an *artistic* medium in worship. Its potential as an art form, however, could not be realized very fully, to our way of

1

thinking, until the *scientific* structure of music was more completely comprehended and developed. The earliest music that does not sound especially strange to our ears is that of the late fifteenth century.

THE ORGAN IN EARLY CHRISTIAN WORSHIP

Instruments called "organs" have been in use since very early times and have been particularly identified with worship practices, although they were used also at feasts and games and even carried into battle for the purpose of confusing and demoralizing the enemy. Acceptance of the organ as an accessory in Christian worship has been neither universal nor immutable. While the Jews were famous for their use of various types of instruments in their Temple services, the early Christians often frowned upon or forbade the use of any kind of instrument.

Clement of Alexandria (150?-215?) said "Only one instrument do we use, *viz.,* the word of peace wherewith we honor God, no longer the old psaltery, trumpet, drum, and flute."

St. Chrysostom (345?-407), considered the greatest orator of the ancient church, had this to say:

> David formerly sang in psalms, also we sing today with him; he had a lyre with lifeless strings, the Church has a lyre with living strings. Our tongues are the strings of the lyre, with a different tone, indeed, with a more accordant piety.

St. Ambrose (340?-397), Bishop of Milan from 374, also opposed the use of instruments, as did St. Augustine. St. Jerome (331?-418) felt that "the Christian maiden ought not even to know what a lyre or a flute is, or what it is used for."

Much of this feeling of antipathy toward the use of instruments in Christian worship resulted from their use in pagan ceremonies and in Roman theatrical productions. This kind of "guilt by association" has appeared from time to time, as we shall see.

Four hundred years before the Reformation the use of organs and instruments in general was severely criticized by Ailred, the Abbot of Rievaulx, when he said:

> Let me speake now of those who, under the show of religion, doe obpalliate the business of pleasure. . . . Whence hath the church so many organs and Musicall Instruments? To what purpose, I pray you, is that terrible noise of blowing of Belloes, expressing rather the crakes of Thunder, than the sweetnesse of a voyce. . . . Why such organs and so many cymbals in the church? What with the sound of

2

the Belloes, the noise of the cymbals, and the united strains of the organ pipes, the common folk stand with wondering faces, trembling and amazed.[1]

THE ORGAN IN SIXTEENTH-CENTURY WORSHIP

As we approach the period of the Reformation, we find that the organ was regularly used in worship services, although in a very limited manner. Its function was mainly to give the tone to the priests and the choir, and it frequently alternated with the latter in the performance of the music. In the sixteenth century, organists tended to take advantage of their position and use the instrument excessively. The Synod of Cambrai, meeting in 1565, decreed that the organ should not be used in this manner in the Creed.

Erasmus (1466-1536), an outstanding Dutch scholar who remained a Catholic even though the Reformation sought to rectify many of the abuses he criticized in his own church, wrote:

There was no music in St. Paul's time. . . . Words nowadays mean nothing. They are mere sounds striking upon the ear, and men are to leave their work and go to church to listen to worse noises than were ever heard in Greek or Roman Theatre. Money must be raised to buy organs and train boys to squeal.[2]

Regarding the polyphonic music which was being widely used in churches at that time, he stated that this was

a tedious and capricious kind of music . . . and a tumultuous noise of different voices. . . . Boys are maintained at great expense . . . a thing that is pestiferous.[3]

The organ has been a source of problems throughout the centuries, both in Roman Catholicism and in the various branches of Protestantism. The former has remained constant in its use of the organ, albeit finding a need periodically to exert pressure on the organist to stay within certain limits. Protestant practice has varied all the way from accepting organs (Lutherans) to demolishing, ruining, and removing them (Calvinists).

Those Protestant church bodies which excluded the use of the organ in their early days have continued to debate the subject heatedly for

[1] William Leslie Sumner, *The Organ* (New York: Philosophical Library, 1952), p. 38.
[2] *Ibid.*, p. 129.
[3] Henry George Farmer, *A History of Music in Scotland* (London: Hinrichsen, 1947), p. 149.

three centuries or more, and even today there are some that do not permit its use in worship. At different periods some groups have found other instruments, such as the bass viol, oboe, bassoon, cello, etc., more acceptable than the organ.

EARLY ORGANS

The use to which church organs were put in the early centuries is not clear. Other instruments, including the kithara, a harp-like instrument, were used as well as the organ. Whatever the need or the purpose, the manufacturing of organs did not get seriously under way until the eighth century, but progress was more rapid in the late ninth and early tenth centuries. While organs were found in churches as early as the sixth century, there is no evidence to show that the organ was used in the music of the Mass until the twelfth century. By the eleventh century it had practically replaced such instruments as the lyre and kithara, which had found some use previous to this. By the thirteenth century the organ had become an integral factor in the performance of the Mass.

From the eleventh to the thirteenth centuries three types of organs were being built: 1) the large organs, generally installed in the galleries of abbeys and cathedrals and in royal establishments; 2) the positive organs, smaller than the large organs but permanently installed; 3) the portative organs, which could be carried by a strap around the neck.

The large organs were not very numerous, although they were built in France, Spain, the Netherlands, Germany, and England. These usually had from sixteen to twenty tones, with several pipes for each tone, and were operated with a wooden slide, which was pushed to let air enter the pipes and pulled to keep it out. By the end of the eleventh century the slides had been replaced by a lever, which was depressed to open the pipe valve and was brought back by a spring to the closed position when the pressure was released. Each lever was from three to five inches wide, was about three feet in length, and had to be depressed a distance of about a foot.

Keyboards were introduced in the thirteenth century. The first keyboards were especially awkward to use because the keys were about as wide as the levers had been, they were a foot in length, and they often had to be depressed as much as two inches to make the pipe speak. The entire hand had to be used to depress a single key. By 1500 the

4

keyboard was more like ours, its narrower keys and lighter action permitting operation by the finger instead of the fist. The keyboard now had four octaves of black and white keys, but the color scheme was the exact opposite of today's customary black-and-white arrangement.

By the end of the fourteenth century, a second set of keys was being added to such large organs as those in the Rouen Cathedral (1386) and the Troyes Cathedral (1422). The number of keys varied from 31 to 47. The second keyboard of the Rouen organ, numbering sixteen keys, could be played independently or coupled to the lower manual. In the early sixteenth century a system of stops was developed, making it possible to select different sets of pipes.

Toward the close of the period presently under consideration, two large organs were installed in Nuremberg. In 1479 the St. Laurence church installed a two-manual organ with 1,100 pipes on the great and 454 on the *positif*. Its longest pipe was thirty-nine feet. The St. Sebald church installed an organ in 1444. Organs of a similar size were installed in France—at Amiens in 1429 and at Rheims in 1487.

The portative organs became quite common in the tenth century. They were used in cathedrals for the performance of miracle and mystery plays, in homes, and in the private chapels of the nobility. Since the portative organ could be played while suspended from a person's neck, it was used for processions both inside and outside the churches. But by the fifteenth century it had lost its popularity because of the impossibility of using it to play part-music. By the seventeenth century it had disappeared from use completely.

A special type of portative organ was the *Regal*, which produced tones by means of reeds instead of pipes. In the mid-sixteenth century a Nuremberg manufacturer built such an instrument in the shape of a large book, which caused it to acquire the epithet of "Bible organ." In Germany it was used to accompany choirs until well into the nineteenth century, and even in more recent times it has been employed to give the pitch for a cappella choirs. Both the portative and the *Regal* were used as much outside the church building as in it, because of their portability.

The third main type of organ, the positive, was smaller than the large organs and could be moved from one location to another, but it could not be played en route. There was a smaller "table model," and there was a larger instrument built to stand on the floor. The smaller type is mentioned as early as the tenth century, but its development was more extensive in the thirteenth. Two persons, using either hands or feet, were required to operate the bellows on this type of organ. It was used both in homes and in churches.

By the fourteenth century the portative and positive organs could play the full chromatic scale, and the portative was replacing the large organ, which was complicated, noisy, and difficult to play. The positive and large organs were often used in combination, with the positive frequently placed behind the player.

Pedals came into use as early as the fourteenth century. The Halberstadt organ, built in 1361, had an octave of pedal keys. The Troyes Cathedral organ in France had a pedalboard of eight keys in 1432, increased to seventeen by the end of the sixteenth century. The first pedals were probably connected to the manual keys and merely pulled them down, rather than operating an independent section of the organ. In 1448 Adam Ileborgh, a German musician-priest of Stendal, wrote the first preludes requiring the real use of pedals. A volume of his organ music, including preludes and other selections, is on display at the Curtis Institute in Philadelphia.

ORGANS IN CENTRAL EUROPE

By the early fifteenth century most of the important churches on the continent had an organ, and some churches had two organs, a larger instrument for solo work and a smaller one for accompanying the singers. By the late sixteenth century the organ had most of the features it has today. German organs of that era had separate pipes for the pedals, two (or even three) keyboards, and couplers. Organ-building and organ music would continue to develop ever higher standards until the early eighteenth century.

The main features of the baroque organ were already to be found on German organs of the early Renaissance. Outside Germany the Renaissance organ was a soft-spoken instrument, usually possessing one manual, and the pedals—if it had any—were of limited range. This was the type of organ most common in Italy and England before the eighteenth century.

German organs of the late Renaissance and baroque periods possessed a wide selection of solo stops (mainly reeds), stops of a more brilliant tone, in most cases two manuals, and a more extensive pedalboard.

6

ORGANS IN OTHER PROTESTANT LANDS

Up to the time of the Reformation, organs in England had only one manual and were either portative or positive organs. There were a few of the larger instruments in existence, such as the Winchester Cathedral organ, built in the tenth century. Slides were used on this instrument to open air passages to the pipes, and there were ten pipes connected to each slide. Since there were forty slides, this meant a total of 400 pipes. Seventy men were required to operate the bellows, and the chief organist had two assistants to operate the slides.

The smaller organs had up to a dozen stops but no pedals. Pedals were generally unknown in England until the latter part of the eighteenth century. Many English churches were not designed with the installation of an organ in mind, perhaps because the English were more interested in singing than in using instruments. The technique of organ-building developed very slowly in England, compared with the progress being made on the Continent.

Numerous churches in the Scandinavian countries had organs by the time of the Reformation. Organs had been introduced to Norway in the eleventh or twelfth century and were used to alternate with the choir, or to play short preludes and postludes. A story is told that prior to 1330 a man came from Iceland with a message for the bishop of Nidaros (now Trondheim) but became so fascinated watching an organ builder at the cathedral that he forgot to deliver it!

Organs were to be found in Denmark before the fourteenth century, and there is evidence that the cathedral in Ribe had an organ about 1300. There are organs still in existence in Denmark and Sweden that were built before 1500. The Uppsala Cathedral had an organ in the thirteenth century. The cathedral in Lund had one from 1317. Sundre had an organ with pedals in 1370. Parts of fourteenth-century organs are on display in the Stockholm National Museum, one of which must have had a 22-key manual and an eight-key pedalboard.

In the thirteenth and early fourteenth centuries organs were forbidden in Sweden and probably in Norway as well, because of the use of organs for secular purposes. There is no record, however, that any organs were removed because of this ban.

ORGAN MUSIC

Since throughout the pre-Reformation period the study, practice, and composition of music was almost wholly an affair of the church and its religious orders, the organists and choir directors of that day were usually priests or monks. And the Catholic and Lutheran organists were usually the best-trained musicians of the early Reformation period. Thus organ music, because of its preeminence, was the first to attain a definite style of composition.

By the end of the fifteenth century there was already a supply of organ literature, prepared by such early composers as Heinrich Isaak, Paulus Hofhaimer, Arnold Schlick, and Conrad Paumann. None of Isaak's organ music is extant, but he is known to have been influential as an organ teacher. Schlick made use of plainsong melodies, with long-note values in the pedal and three-part counterpoint for the manual. This type of music remained in common use for two and a half centuries. Hofhaimer was widely known as a performer and a teacher, and several of his pupils became illustrious performers. Paumann prepared an instruction book in counterpoint for organists, published 1452.

Of the quantity of organ music books available in the early sixteenth century, one of the most famous was Sebastian Virdung's *Musica Getutscht* of 1511. Instruction books and collections of organ music began to multiply as the century progressed, and instrumental music received its first definite style forms.

When the Reformation began, early in the sixteenth century, organ music composition and organ performance were on firm ground. During the next two centuries the Lutheran chorale was to complement these other achievements and give to organ music an immense depth and breadth of expression.

EARLY VOCAL CHURCH MUSIC

THE CHOIR IN PRE-REFORMATION WORSHIP

While most early Christians would seem to have rejected the use of instruments for worship purposes, the choir soon became a specialized group. After the Edict of Milan in 313 the persecution of Christians ceased and they were permitted to worship publicly, which gave impetus to the matter of training choirs to help celebrate the Mass. Special schools were established for this purpose, and the singers were given the status of lesser clergy.

Up to this time a certain amount of congregational singing had been a characteristic feature of Christian worship. With the establishment of a trained choir, the singing of the Mass eventually became the province of clergy and choir, and thereafter the congregation did not actively participate. By the end of the sixth century this was a confirmed tradition of church music.

POLYPHONIC CHORAL MUSIC

From the eleventh through the fourteenth centuries the entire field of church music was enlarged through the development of polyphony, which permitted choirs to sing music in parts, whereas until then it had been limited exclusively to the chanting of a single melodic line. The printing of music came into vogue about 1500, and by that time there was also an adequate and accurate system of musical notation. Previous attempts at using part music had been tedious, erratic, and highly experimental, awaiting the time when a more scientific basis for the art could be established. By the twelfth century the technique of part-writing had developed to the point where intervals of thirds and sixths were preferred over fourths and fifths, and dissonances with satisfying resolutions were being employed.

As advances in this type of composition were made, the newly found freedom in part music often led singers to extemporize their parts, adding embellishments and frills beyond all bounds of reason. When this practice was indulged in by singers possessing voice and imagination but no understanding of the intricacies of musical structure, only confusion could result. A learned theorist of the fourteenth century, Jean de Muris, had this to say about such practices:

> How can men have the face to sing discant who know nothing of the combination of sounds! Their voices roam around the *cantus firmus* [main theme] without regard to any rule; they throw their tones out by luck, just as an unskilled thrower hurls a stone, hitting the mark once in a hundred casts. . . . O roughness, O bestiality! taking an ass for a man, a kid for a lion, a sheep for a fish. They cannot tell a consonance from a dissonance. They are like a blind man trying to strike a dog.[4]

Another writer asked,

> Does such oxen bellowing belong in the church? Is it believed that God can be graciously inclined by such an uproar? [5]

Other writers of the period described singers who would put their

---

[4] Edward Dickinson, *Music in the History of the Western Church* (New York: Scribner's, 1923), p. 146.
[5] *Ibid.,* p. 146.

bodies, limbs, eyes, etc., through contortions which must have resembled those of contemporary rock-and-roll singers.

By the fifteenth century the music that the choirs were singing was of a very high caliber and would not sound particularly out of place today. Five centuries of part-writing technique was steadily and surely pressing toward its culmination in the incomparable sixteenth-century works of Palestrina.

As the Roman liturgy developed, so did the need for a choir. For centuries the choir was made responsible for the more important responses of the Mass: Kyrie, Gloria in Excelsis, Credo, Sanctus et Benedictus, and Agnus Dei. Only in very recent times have Roman Catholic liturgical practices permitted the congregation to replace the choir in singing these sections of the liturgy.

CHORAL TRAINING

A very common practice of the pre-Reformation German municipalities was to maintain schools where choirs could be trained for the church service. The town paid the bill to keep boys with good voices in school, and in this way they received much (or even all) of their education. Besides singing in the choir the boys learned to play an instrument, so that once their voices had changed they could play in the orchestra that frequently accompanied the choir. Students with the proper qualifications could continue their studies at the university, if they lived in a university city. Instruction in music, therefore, became a vital part of the educational program. This is why so many educated men of the time were also musicians or knew quite a bit about music. The pattern persisted, in fact, until the time of J. S. Bach.

CHORAL MUSIC IN ENGLAND AND SCANDINAVIA

English church musicians were also avid promoters of polyphonic music. Each monastery and abbey was a school of music, where boy choristers received musical instruction from the monks in conjunction with their academic education, and this educational system received very adequate support. Among the leading English composers who wrote for the Roman Church services were Thomas Tallis, Christopher Tye, and Robert Whyte. These men did not need to imitate the Italian composers, e.g., di Lasso and Palestrina, since England had already established its own traditions of music composition. But during the Reformation much of their music fell into disuse.

A curious English custom of this period was that of giving the choir boys liberty to fine anyone who entered a church wearing spurs, because of the jingling sound these made. Even members of royalty were not exempt from this playful regulation. Henry VIII's expense record reveals that on October 1, 1485 (the first year of his kingship), he had paid a fine of four shillings to the boys "for the King's spoures."

This practice was later given an educational turn, when in 1622 the Dean of the Chapel Royal decreed that

> if any Knight or other person entituled to wear spurs, enter ye Chappell in that guise, he shall pay to ye quiristers ye accustomed fine; but if he command ye youngest quirister to repeat hys "gamut," [6] and he faile in ye so doing, the said Knight or other, shall not pay ye fine.[7]

England, like the Continent, had its share of church music critics. The following evaluation is by the abbot of Rivaulx Abbey in Yorkshire:

> This man sings a base, that a small meane, another a treble, a fourth divides and cuts asunder, as it were, certain middle notes. One while the voyse is strained, anon it is remitted, now it is dashed, and then againe it is inlarged with a lowder sound. Sometimes, which is a shame to speake, it is enforced into a horse's neighings; sometimes, the masculine vigour being laid aside, it is sharpened into the shrilnesse of a woman's voyce. . . . Sometimes thou may'st see a man with an open mouth, not to sing, but, as it were, to breathe out his last gaspe, by shutling in his breath, and by a certaine ridiculous interception of his voyce, as it were to threaten silence, and now again to imitate the agonies of a dying man . . . the common people standing by, trembling and astonished, admire the sound of the Organs, the noyse of the Cymbals and Musicall Instruments, the harmony of the Pipes and Cornets.[8]

Church choirs that had come into existence in pre-Reformation Scandinavia were for the most part disbanded under the Reformation and combined with the Latin schools. In this era the Scandinavians lacked a musical culture of their own, which meant they had to draw heavily upon the musical resources of Germany in the early centuries of the Reformation period.

---

[6] The order of the notes in the Guidonian hexachordal system, which consisted of six-note scales.

[7] John S. Bumpus, *History of English Cathedral Music 1549-1889* (London: T. Werner Laurie, 1908), p. 106.

[8] Archibald T. Davidson, *Church Music—Illusion and Reality* (Cambridge: Harvard Univ. Press, 1952), pp. 45, 46.

11

As we narrow our focus in the following pages to the music of Protestantism, we will do well to remember the words of a well-known music historian:

> In the Middle Age, we are told, religion and art lived together in brotherly union; Protestantism threw away art and kept religion, Renaissance rationalism threw away religion and retained art. In painting and sculpture this is very nearly the truth; in music it is very far from being true. It is the glory of the art of music that she has almost always been able to resist the drift toward sensuousness and levity, and where she has apparently yielded, her recovery has been speedy and sure. So susceptible is her very nature to the finest touches of religious feeling, that every revival of the pure spirit of devotion has always found her prepared to adapt herself to new spiritual demands, and out of apparent decline to develop forms of religious expression more beautiful and sublime even than the old.[9]

[9] Edward Dickinson, *op. cit.*, pp. 272, 273.

II

The Early
Reformation Period

IN GERMANY

The task of following our subject through the first centuries of the Reformation will be encumbered by the divisiveness that plagued the general movement, the "reformations within the Reformation" led by such men as John Calvin, Ulrich Zwingli, and John Knox. Our first concern, however, will be to trace Martin Luther's influence on church music and to see what happened within the geographical limits of Germany.

LUTHER AND CHURCH MUSIC

The Lutheran reformers had one main working principle: to alter and adapt the existing practices to fit their own particular concepts, which meant that they did not immediately assign new duties to choir or organ, nor did they restrict them, as did other branches of Protestantism. The traditional forms of early sixteenth-century Roman music were retained and allowed to develop gradually into the forms that would give a particular identification to the new faith. Thus in Luther's first order of worship, the *Formula Missae* of 1535, the musical elements corresponded with those of the Roman Catholic Mass.

Luther was not the least bit naïve when it came to church music, for as a monk he had been trained in this subject. He also lived near such music centers as Erfurt, Leipzig, Torgau, and Wittenberg, and in his home there were often informal performances of music by such composers as Josquin Deprès, Johann Walther, Ludwig Senfl, and others.

13

He even had enough familiarity with the contrapuntal technique of his time to do some amateur composing of his own.

Luther was interested in music—especially choral music—as an art, and he sought its artistic development in the church. As far as the organ was concerned, he must have been thoroughly imbued with the Roman church's attitude toward the instrument, which was more a matter of toleration than of encouragement. He probably felt that the organ made no significant contribution to the service, for he never mentioned it as a liturgical necessity. His *Formula Missae,* his *Deutsche Messe,* and the Wittenberg Church Orders of 1533 and 1559 made no mention of the organ, even though it was played freely in the Wittenberg services. Luther once made the not-very-complimentary remark that

> there can be more faith in a miller lad than in all the Papists, and it can avail more than all the Popes and monks with their organs and tricks, even had they more organs than there are pipes therein.[1]

And the Council of Trent (1545-63) also placed severe restrictions on the use of the organ in Roman Catholic worship.

Nevertheless, Luther's writings clearly indicate that he was interested in the arts, particularly music, so long as these served the church. He did not think—as did some other Reformers—that the arts should be removed from worship. And he was particularly interested in retaining music as an integral part of the church service.

Nor was his interest restricted to congregational singing, in which he was vitally interested; it also included the polyphonic choral music of his day. While he allowed for the fact that some people did not understand the niceties of choral artistry, he felt nevertheless that the beauty and splendor of fine music deserved a place in the worship service. Music was a gift of God and should not be ignored.

He characterized polyphonic music as "a heavenly dance," in which the voices "skip delightedly" around the main melody, sung, as a rule, by the tenor.

On the basis of his writings and his own participation in church music affairs, we can only conclude that Luther saw music as a useful ally in the implementation of his reforms, which in the areas of church music had a three-prong thrust: (1) the use of the choir, (2) the

---

[1] G. W. Stewart, *Music in Church Worship* (London: Hodder and Stoughton, 1926), p. 230.

congregational hymn, and (3) the unison chant. The first and last of these were brought over from the liturgy of the Roman church. The distinctly new element was the congregational hymn.

In contrast to his indifference regarding the organ, Luther had some very definite things to say about the choir, which he considered almost obligatory in the new order of service. The choir, for him, fulfilled two main functions: to lead congregational singing and to sing compositions that would add beauty to the service. There is really nothing we can add to this concept after better than four hundred years of Protestant worship! It was Luther's wish, where possible, to have two choirs: a smaller group to sing the first part of the petitions and a larger one to lead the congregation in singing the responses. Where this was not possible, the first part was read by the pastor, as is still done in many Lutheran churches today.

Whether the special compositions sung by the choir were written by a Catholic or a Lutheran composer was a matter of small concern to Luther. He only asked that the music be appropriate for the worship of God. He felt, however, that the choir should not monopolize the musical element of congregational worship but that the congregation should also take an active part in singing the chorales and other sections of the liturgy. Wherever the congregation did not take part, Luther tried to keep the music identical with the Roman service, because of its desirable devotional qualities.

The importance of the congregational hymn in the early German Lutheran churches should not be overrated. Hymns were for the most part sung at home in private devotions, at school by the students, and by cantors. The only exception was the small congregation that had no choir, in which case the congregational hymn was often used to replace the parts of the Mass normally sung by the choir. And what few songs the congregation could sing had to be memorized, because they did not take their hymnbooks to church with them.

In any case, the organ was not used to accompany either the choir or the congregation, since at that time there was no organ music suitable for this purpose. The only support for congregational singing, then, was the choir. But if the choir was not available, the congregation sang more, and if there was a choir they sang much less, almost not at all. When the choir did sing, it was probably in Latin, because the musical settings available were written to accompany Latin texts. It was only by the mid-seventeenth century—one hundred fifty years after the Reformation began—that congregational singing became a generally accepted practice.

THE USE OF THE ORGAN

In both the Roman Catholic and the early Lutheran churches the organ played a short prelude to introduce each musical section of the service, which was then rendered by the priest or the choir. The organ also alternated with the choir in the liturgical choir numbers. In such instances, the organ played its parts alone and did not accompany the choir. Protestant use of the organ did not essentially vary from Catholic usage during the first hundred years of the Reformation. If the congregation sang, the organ also alternated with the congregation. (The congregation sang through a stanza, after which the organ played it through once.) The organ introduced the main parts of the service—Introit, Kyrie, Agnus Dei, etc.—and then (usually) alternated with the choir as it sang these selections. Congregational participation was probably not a very strong factor in most cases. The organ was the important musical medium, since it introduced most of the vocal pieces, whether sung by priest, choir, or congregation.

Sometimes there was joint participation in the chorales by congregation, choir, and organ. First the congregation sang a stanza unaccompanied, then the choir sang a polyphonic setting of the same chorale, after which the organ had its turn to play a solo. It was not felt purposeless to have the organ played in this manner, since the congregation had memorized what few hymns they used, and they could think through the words of a stanza while the organ was playing its part.

From time to time organists have become discontented with the restrictions imposed upon them because of the very nature of a worship service. There was this unrest also in the early sixteenth century, when it became a practice among organists to employ special devices, such as injecting quick-running passages into their preludes, or even playing secular tunes. In 1548 an organist in Strasbourg was dismissed from his post for having played French and Italian songs during the offertory. At times, also, the organist infringed upon the normal function of the choir by playing some of its parts of the liturgy. The refinements of early sixteenth-century organ manufacturing would have contributed also to giving the organist "itchy fingers" and the desire to expand his domain of performance. Thus throughout the sixteenth century the organist was the target of numerous criticisms. He was constantly being asked not to play secular music in church and not to play parts for which he was not needed. Frequently, both Lutheran and Catholic organists would play for Sunday service some of the secular music used at home.

Continued refinements in organ manufacture throughout the sixteenth century and the general growth of music as an artistic medium engendered a feeling that, whatever the possible invidiousness of the situation, the organist would have to be given more time for independent performance. In 1597 the theological faculty at Wittenberg expressed itself as being in favor of more time for the organ, believing that this was just one more medium through which the human heart might find joy, courage, and other Christian attributes. They suggested, however, that the sermon should not be shortened in order to give more time to the organ.

The organ could not be used to accompany congregational singing, because the technique of musical composition had until then been basically vocal. The interweaving of parts that was so characteristic of choral polyphony could not be adapted to the accompaniment of congregational singing, since the latter required harmonization of each individual note of the chorale melody in a vertical harmonic structure. Before this was accomplished, it would be necessary for musical composition technique to push beyond the centuries-old contrapuntal system to a newer concept of harmony. But that belongs to a later period of our history.

THE FUNCTION OF THE CHOIR

As has already been indicated, Luther retained the choir for the main parts of the service. The function of the choir in the early Lutheran service was almost the same as in the Roman Catholic. The Lutheran choir sang the Kyrie, Gloria in Excelsis, Sanctus et Benedictus, and Agnus Dei, up through the time of J. S. Bach. In the smaller churches where no choir was available, the congregation, in addition to the Kyrie, sang the following hymns instead: *Gott Vater in Ewigkeit, Allein Gott in der Höh sei Ehr, Wir Glauben all an einen Gott, Jesaia dem Propheten das geschah,* and *O Lamm Gottes unschuldig.* And in the absence of a choir, the pastor sometimes read those parts of the service usually sung by the choir.

Besides singing the main parts of the liturgy, the choir, rather than the organ, was responsible for leading congregational singing, in view of the latter's inability to perform this function. The first experiments in organ accompaniment were not very successful, leading to its abandonment by the middle of the sixteenth century. It remained for the Nuremberg musician-pastor Lukas Osiander to develop (in 1586) a much better method, which will be described presently.

It was Luther's intention that the special choir numbers, always based on chorale melodies, should be sung by the choir while the congregation joined in on the melody. But this did not work out, because of the complexity of the polyphonic structure and the practice of assigning the chorale melody to the tenor or alto voice rather than to the soprano, thus making it difficult for the congregation to follow their part. The *Church Choral Book,* prepared by Luther and his chief music assistant Johann Walther, was published in Wittenberg in 1524 and contained a collection of these compositions, written for a choir of four or five parts and with the melody in the tenor. Only those members of the congregation who felt musically sure of themselves would attempt to sing along with the choir. Occasionally a choir would sing the chorale melody in unison, but this practice apparently did not prevail. In the absence of a choir it became the duty of the cantor to lead congregational singing.

The use of the choir in this manner did not accomplish very much in the promotion of congregational singing. It became clear that both the choir and the organ would have to be better utilized if the situation was to improve. What was needed was a new type of music, in which each note of the chorale melody would have its own harmonic structure and the movement of the various parts would for the most part coincide with that of the melody. The more involved type of contrapuntal music that had evolved over the centuries was not meeting this requirement.

A new stage in the development of choir-led congregational singing was inaugurated by Lukas Osiander, who in 1586 published his *Fünfzig geistliche Lieder.* The purpose of this collection is evident from a translation of the full title: "Fifty spiritual songs and psalms for four voices, arranged in such a way that the whole congregation may fully participate in singing them." Osiander initiated a simple four-part harmonization in which the chorale melody was carried by the soprano and the other parts moved with it in an almost note-for-note accompaniment, making it possible for the congregation to follow the choir and thus giving a decided impetus to the cause of congregational

18

singing. Even though this volume was slanted for use by the choir, the German church music historian Friedrich Zelle has called this "the first evangelical chorale-book." [2] Now that there was a new technique in musical composition that made *harmony* the dominating structural element instead of *counterpoint,* the stage was set for the organ to take over its function of accompanying the congregation in the chorales. An intermediate step was taken in this direction when the organist, in the absence of a choir, accompanied congregational singing in a simple counterpoint, just as the lute had been used to accompany singing in the homes. It was nothing new for the organist to play the chorale melodies, in view of this long-standing secular tradition of instrumental accompaniment, which consisted of playing the melody and adding a few ornamentations.

As congregational singing became more firmly established, the need for the choir to assist the congregation was lessened, and the task of accompanying the congregation was left entirely to the organ. It would take most of the seventeenth (and in many localities until the eighteenth) century for this transition to be fully realized.

Most of the polyphonic choral compositions had been intended for unaccompanied singing. At times, however, a kind of accompaniment was used that the score did not call for. The organ commonly assisted in some manner, and on festival occasions it was supplemented with flutes, cornets, lutes, and other string instruments. The sixteenth-century musicians were a practical lot and frequently sang without accompaniment, but they did not hesitate to call upon the organist for assistance or to use whatever other instruments might be available, sometimes to help the singers perform with a greater confidence, sometimes to provide a wider variety of tonal color.

A very excellent choral training program was carried on in the parochial and cathedral schools. Boys from the lower classes often sang for church services and for such special occasions as weddings, baptisms, and funerals. Because so many of these boys were from poor families, the schools admitted them on the basis of their musical ability. A portion of the money received for their special services was divided between the singers at the end of each week, and the remainder was held in trust until the end of the term. J. S. Bach was later to be one of the beneficiaries of this type of program.

In the higher Latin schools the choir boys also served in the orches-

---

[2] See No. 217 in the bibliography.

tra when instrumental accompaniment was required. Such older students were called "alumni," and when their voices changed they sang tenor and bass, while the younger boys with unchanged voices sang the treble parts. These groups did a considerable amount of eight-part singing, and in exchange for their services received room and board, candles, and firewood. The funds for operating these schools came mainly from people who were interested in church music. Although a pre-Reformation practice to begin with, it was continued by the Lutherans. Many students received enough musical training in these schools to become professional musicians.

The smaller town had its *Kantorei,* a volunteer singing organization that placed itself at the service of the church. A considerable percentage of *Kantorei* activities were social in nature, but the group frequently participated in special church events. The adult members of the *Kantorei* were generally those who had been choir boys as youngsters. They sang the tenor and bass parts while the younger members sang the soprano and alto. The group also supplied its own instrumental accompaniment as needed. Wealthy citizens often provided financial support.

By the close of the sixteenth century the Lutherans had developed well-defined orders of service, both for the cathedral service and for the simpler rites of the small congregation. During this period the cantor in the smaller congregation frequently took work outside the church in order to support himself. Sometimes this meant serving as dance organist in the local tavern.

By the end of this century, Lutheran church music had also earned a place for itself in the world of music, for by this time it had grown independent of Roman Catholic music, both in technique and in practice, having distinguished itself by the use of chorale melodies in its vocal and instrumental music.

IN SCANDINAVIA

Until comparatively recent times the Scandinavian countries were united by very close political relationships.[3] Denmark and parts of Sweden have had a closer geographical affinity with the mainland, so

---

[3] Denmark, Norway, and Sweden were united in 1397 with the Union of Kalmar. They continued under one monarch until 1523, at which time Sweden became a separate monarchy. The Norwegians continued subject to the King of Denmark until 1814, when Norway became affiliated with Sweden, from whom she gained complete independence in 1905.

that these areas were in contact earlier with the cultural influences coming from more southern lands. The Christianization of Scandinavia was well under way by the early twelfth century, and by the middle of that century churches, monasteries, and convents had been established. Of course, any attempt to impose the Latin language and culture on these hardy Scandinavian peoples was not without its difficulties. During the changeover to Lutheranism the cathedral schools of the Catholic era were combined with the Reformation-style Latin schools. At the dawn of the Reformation there were Scandinavian churches here and there that possessed organs.

Sweden proved a favorable climate, not only to the Reformation, but to Protestant church music. Gustav I, who became the first Swedish monarch after his country's withdrawal from the Union of Kalmar, was both a lover of Protestantism and a lover of music. The first Swedish Lutheran hymnal was published in 1526, and the Swedish Mass, like Luther's German Mass, included songs for the congregation to sing. With the adoption of the Confession of Augsburg in 1593, Sweden severed all remaining connections with the Roman service.

The Church Order of 1571, commenting on the role of the pastor and choir in the service, asked on behalf of the best interests of the congregation that the songs should not always be in Latin. The transition to a vernacular liturgy came slowly for both the pastors and the choirs, undoubtedly because of the absence of musical settings for Swedish texts. An item from 1575, however, mentions that the choir sang in Swedish.

Denmark and Norway got their first hymnal in 1569—Hans Thomisson's *Psalmebog*. Nils Jesperson's *Gradual* of 1573, which the organists presumably used in some manner, contained only melodies. A few choirs were organized in this period.

Church music in these northern countries fared poorly throughout the first century of the Reformation. The Scandinavians were not always too appreciative of the fine arts, and considerable portions of the population were illiterate. If there was a great deal of resentment against the Roman Church for introducing the Latin language into the service, there was even more hostility against the smoothly flowing Gregorian chants, which seemed out of place in this harsher Nordic world.

Even before the Reformation there had been attempts to do away with the organ, particularly in Sweden. Antipathy to the instrument carried over into the early period of the Reformation, when its use was forbidden. In fact, many organs were removed and destroyed.

To add insult to injury, the Reformation was forced upon the people by their rulers—Gustav I in Sweden and Christian III in Denmark and Norway. Almost overnight Catholic priests renounced celibacy, became Lutheran pastors, married, and raised large families on meager salaries. Some of them were not very good pastors. They led questionable lives, were involved in drunken brawls, lived in open immorality; some were even murderers. Life was primitive here, especially in the more remote regions. Parishioners frequently became hostile to the church and even offered to pay the government *not* to have a pastor. One young man boasted that his father had killed three preachers, and in a drunken stupor he prayed that he might match his father's record.

These matters are not a commentary on church music, of course. They merely indicate why there was little of it in the sixteenth century. A few organs were actually installed in Sweden where, despite the earlier opposition, conditions became more favorable and more progress was made than in the rest of Scandinavia. Denmark had very few musical instruments. There are records of a positive organ being installed in the Nidaros Cathedral at Trondheim, Norway, in 1593.

Not until the seventeenth century would Scandinavians make much visible progress in church music.

IN SWITZERLAND

ZWINGLI

In 1518 Zwingli began preaching the plain gospel truth at Zürich, which led to disputations with the vicar-general of the Bishop of Constance. As a result, images and the Mass were to be swept away as the new theological movement spread over most of Switzerland. Zwingli met with Luther and other reformers in 1529, and they discovered many points of theological agreement.

Zwingli's break with Rome was not without acrimony, and for this reason he came to oppose almost everything the Roman Church stood for, including its music. Though personally a friend of music and, like Luther, somewhat talented—he had composed a melody to accompany his versification of the 129th Psalm—Zwingli was at first adamantly opposed to music in the church. It was his conviction that neither organ nor choir had a rightful place in the service, and what liturgy he employed did not call for sung responses but for spoken responses by the congregation.

At the time of the Reformation a number of student choirs were active in Switzerland. In earlier times they had performed choral compositions at worship services, and still later they had accompanied congregational singing. Since church music, as Zwingli knew it, was inseparably connected with the Roman liturgy—of which he wanted no part—and since the choral texts were in Latin, which made them unintelligible to the people he served, he suspended choir singing in 1525 and two years later had the Zürich Cathedral organ destroyed. Lang describes the destruction of the organs in both Zürich and Bern:

> The Cathedral organist in Zürich watched, with tears streaming down his cheeks, the destruction of his magnificent instrument; and the famous Bern organist, Hans Kotter, made homeless by his unwavering faith in Protestantism, saw himself reduced to the status of a schoolteacher when the very champions of his faith destroyed his instrument.[4]

Commenting on the polyphonic choral music of the time, Zwingli said that

> the roaring in the churches, scarce understood by the priests themselves, is a foolish and vain abuse, and a most pernicious hindrance to piety.[5]

Some Swiss congregations—not Zwingli's—practiced congregational singing during the second quarter of the sixteenth century. And if Zwingli had not come to an untimely death at the age of forty-seven, it is quite possible even he would have begun restoring music to his worship services. This is hinted at in his communion liturgy of 1525, where he stated that singing by the choir and congregation might well be justified. Another seventy-three years were to pass, however, before the ruling authorities would permit such singing.

CALVIN

At the age of 23, John Calvin, a brilliant French scholar, became so impressed by the doctrines of the Reformation in Germany that he was led to use his influence in behalf of the movement in Paris, now a center of the "new learning." So intense was the feeling against the small band of French Protestants that persecution broke out, and

---

[4] Paul Henry Lang, *Music in Western Civilization* (New York: W. W. Norton, 1941), pp. 208, 209.
[5] Henry George Farmer, *op. cit.,* p. 149.

Calvin had to flee to Basel, Switzerland, where in 1536, at the age of 25, he issued his famous *Institutes of the Christian Religion.*

Like Zwingli, Calvin had a personal interest in music, but he had grave reservations about its use in church. He felt that the polyphonic music of the time could be used by groups meeting in homes, but he did not agree with the Lutherans that it was appropriate for worship services, feeling rather that it detracted from the spiritual message. The singing of polyphonic music was especially popular in Switzerland at that time, and composers such as Claude Goudimel and Jacques Mauduit had so perfected their technique that their works compared favorably with the motets being produced outside Calvin's sphere of influence.

The Calvinistic churches in Switzerland and in western and southern Germany discarded their organs. The church in Heidelberg, for example, had no organ from 1570 until 1652.

Meanwhile the Roman church was having its own difficulties with organs. The Council of Trent (1545-1563) enjoined Catholics not to attend churches where the organ was used or where the singing was so "lewd or impure" that it defiled the house of God.

The organ was reintroduced in Basel just after the middle of the century, at a time when the city was inclining more toward Lutheranism, but in 1640 it was again condemned to silence for a couple of years.

IN THE NETHERLANDS

Unlike the Scandinavian countries and Switzerland, the Netherlands occupied a position of preeminence in the musical world before the Reformation ever began. Such illustrious composers as Guillaume Dufay (1400?-1474), Johannes Okeghem (1430?-1495), and Josquin Deprès (1450?-1521) managed during their lifetime to give the Netherlands a position of leadership in the musical world. Only England (possibly France) [6] could lay claim to any such distinction, thanks to the work of John Dunstable (d. 1453), whom music historians generally refer to as "the first composer."

Martin Luther himself had a particular fondness for the compositions of the Flemish composer Deprès. And before the Reformation reached the Netherlands the work of Orlando Lasso (1530?-1594) had also reached its maturity.

---

[6] Since Dunstable was better known on the Continent than in England, one may suppose that he spent much of his time in France.

With all this rich musical heritage one would have expected the Dutch Reformed Church, organized in 1568 at the Synod of Wezel, to be at least tolerantly disposed toward music in the church. As Dutchmen they were apparently so disposed, but as theologians just returned from studying in Geneva, they were piping Calvin's tune.

Since a pre-Reformation tradition consigned church organs and organists to the care of the town councils rather than to the church officials, these latter did not succeed in removing the organs, even though the official position of the Reformed Church demanded it. Considerably more pressure was brought to bear when the Calvin-oriented clergy returned, and at the Synod of Dordrecht in 1574 it was agreed that the playing of organs in the churches must be utterly abolished. In some municipalities this decision was implemented, but in other instances the town council held out against it.

The Synod of Dordrecht in 1578 reiterated the ban on organs, as did the Synod of Middleburg three years later—clear indications that a number of churches still possessed these instruments. Realizing that their fight was futile, the Synod of Edam in 1586 decided that if any church was still concerned about the playing of "unseemly and worldly songs on bells and organs," they should consult with the city authorities and seek to improve the situation.

Since the organ remained silent during the church service proper, the town council frequently required its organist to play an hour-long recital following the close of the service, and sometimes a half-hour recital before the service began. Members of the congregation often objected to having a recital at the close of the service, saying that it made them forget what they had heard in the sermon.

The Dutch reformers also had little interest in choral music, and even the great choral compositions of their own countrymen were not used in church. The church choir was simply nonexistent.

IN SCOTLAND

By the fifteenth century the Roman Church was firmly established in Scotland, and the nation [7] was divided into thirteen dioceses. John Knox (1505?-1572) left Scotland about the middle of the century and studied for some time in Geneva under John Calvin. Returning in 1559, he was largely instrumental in making Protestantism the

---

[7] Scotland and England did not become one country until the Act of Union in 1707.

national faith of the land. The following year, in fact, the Scotch Parliament adopted a *Confession of Faith* that Knox had prepared.

Scotch Protestantism followed the Calvinistic pattern of Geneva, which meant that the churches were purged of all "popish stuff," including service books, mass books, vestments, etc. Often these items were cast into the streets, gathered into heaps, and burned. It is probable that what few organs had been placed in Scotch churches before this time were also removed or destroyed. The few that escaped such a fate would not have been used. In 1574 the Session of Aberdeen decreed that all organs be removed from the churches and that the money realized from their sale be used for the poor. The five organs at the Chapel Royal were also destroyed, and the chaplains, choristers, and musicians were discharged.

Some Scotch Reformation leaders were not even sure that the simple psalmody of Calvin should be used. Polyphonic choral music was considered "mere vanity." Thomas Wood, vicar at St. Andrews, prepared a psalter with part-music settings in 1562-66, but it was not published and may not have been used to any degree. Part-singing may well have been an activity carried on outside the time of formal worship, but the church gave no official or unofficial approval or encouragement to the use of organs, choirs, or part-singing.

Whereas by the end of the sixteenth century most of the strong feelings against the organ had died out in England, in Scotland they lingered on. The Anglicans were thus much more favorably inclined toward its use than were the Scotch Presbyterians.

IN ENGLAND

In England, as much as on the Continent, the Reformation was a divided movement, with Anglicanism (the Church of England) pitted against a more austere element, Puritanism. Something of this ancient cleavage is still recognizable today. The Puritans, active from the very beginning, felt that the Anglicans had not broken sufficiently with the Roman pattern of worship. Later they felt the reforms under Elizabeth were also inadequate. From 1649 to 1660 they enjoyed a period of political supremacy, but after the Act of Uniformity (1662) they once more became a dissenting minority.

In contrast to Protestant beginnings in Germany, Switzerland, the Netherlands, and Scotland, the English Reformation was not initiated by commoners like Luther, Zwingli, Calvin, or Knox, but began at the top (as it had in Scandinavia) with King Henry VIII (1509-47). Henry had not been experiencing too cordial relations with Rome for a while, and finally decided that the thing to do was to assume supreme ecclesiastical leadership in his own country, thus breaking with the papacy.

In view of Henry's highhanded methods, some prefer to locate the beginnings of the English Reformation during the reign of his son, Edward VI. Since Edward was born to Henry by his third wife, one could argue, of course, that there would have been no Edward VI to start the Reformation if Henry had not broken with the Pope in order to remarry.

At any rate, it was under Edward that the first Protestant prayer book [8] was formulated and put into use. The five-year regression to Catholicism under Queen Mary was not a serious setback to the onward march of the Reformation. To help the reader grasp the complexities of the situation, we show here a table indicating the contributions to the Reformation made by Henry VIII and the Tudor monarchs who succeeded him:

Ruler	*Period*	*Accomplishments*
Henry VIII	1509-1547	Reformation started
Edward VI	1547-1553	First Prayer Book prepared, 1549
		Second Prayer Book issued, 1552
Mary	1553-1558	Reversion to Catholicism
Elizabeth	1558-1603	Reformation reestablished
		Prayer Book of 1559 issued

With the death of Queen Elizabeth the Stuart family of Scotland took over the throne of England and retained it until 1714, except during the Puritan interlude. What historians call the Restoration refers to the reestablishment of the Stuart dynasty after the fall of the Puritans.

We mention all these details of English political history because they have some bearing on our subject: the ruling families of that age exercised considerable influence on church music policies. The Tudors, for instance, were musically educated people who gave both moral and material patronage to the fine arts. During the Tudor era,

---

[8] We ought to point out here that what Anglicans call the Prayer Book, i.e., the *Book of Common Prayer,* is not just a collection of prayers but a presentation of the Anglican liturgy.

therefore, church music flourished. The Stuarts, on the other hand, cared little about music in general and even less about church music, which could account for the fact that English music from 1660 to 1900 lagged behind that of the Continent, and that England made no significant contributions to church music during this period.

Before the Reformation got under way in England, the Roman Catholics had six hundred monasteries and convents serving the church, each with a musical establishment that included a choir and one or more organists. When the Reformers did away with daily celebration of the Mass, many of the cathedrals and collegiate churches tried to maintain the same sort of musical program that they had operated under Catholicism. English versions of the Mass were immediately substituted for the Latin, and these continued in use until the publication of the Book of Common Prayer, after which composers began using texts from this new liturgy for their special compositions. Before long the Choral Matins and the Evensong—the latter particularly loved by English and foreigners alike—had won their places in the Anglican service.

THE EARLY REFORMATION CHOIRS

The pre-Reformation polyphonic music was widely discontinued by the English Reformation, since the reformers were personally opposed to it. In 1544 Thomas Cranmer, archbishop of Canterbury, stated in his famous letter on the litany that it was

> required that the elaborate and intricate polyphony of the time should be discarded and replaced by a simple close-fitting music which should set one note to each syllable and so allow the words be clearly heard and understood.[9]

This instruction was followed closely for some time. But the large music establishments, for example, the Cathedral choirs, the Royal Chapel choirs, and the Collegiate Chapel choirs—such as those at Oxford and Cambridge Universities—were not much disturbed by the change to Protestantism. These continued functioning without a real break. After the middle of the sixteenth century, however, the clergy became opposed to the use of choirs, reduced the number of singers, and even redirected into other channels the money allocated for maintaining the musical program.

---

[9] Sir W. H. Hadow, *Church Music* (London: Longmans, Green, 1926), p. 20.

The Church of England adopted a sensible basic program for its church music, a plan which by and large is still in use today. Recognizing that musical capabilities vary from one congregation to another, they adopted three forms of worship:

a. The Choral Service, mainly for the large establishments—cathedrals, collegiate chapels, and chapels royal. This service included chants and an anthem.
b. The Parochial Service, for churches which did not have a choir, hence, no chants or anthem.
c. The Mixed Service, where a choir of some capability was available and could sing some parts of the service.

As a part of this program composers started writing what were called "short services" and "great services." William Byrd, the "English Palestrina" (c. 1543-1623), introduced the use of the solo voice, accompanied by the organ, into his short service. Some composers utilized both duet and solo passages to the accompaniment of the choir. Great services were written by composers such as Byrd; Tallis (ca. 1520-1585); Gibbons (1583-1625), who was considered the foremost of English composers and organists; and Morley (1557-1603). The "great service" musical settings were more involved and employed the older contrapuntal technique alongside newer harmony patterns just then coming into use.

England's best composers wrote for the church. Admittedly, it could be a bit confusing to write first for the Roman ritual, then for the Anglican, to return to the Roman under Mary and once more to the Anglican under Elizabeth. Byrd never left his first faith, but Christopher Tye (died 1572—sometimes referred to as "the father of the anthem") and Thomas Tallis (composer of Tallis' Canon) could change their musical colors like chameleons to satisfy the religious feelings of each succeeding monarch, apparently to the complete satisfaction of both camps.

Composers had their troubles, of course. John Marbeck (or Merbecke) a contemporary of Tallis, narrowly escaped burning at the stake because of his sympathies with the Reformation. John Taverner, an Oxford organist and composer, was not persecuted for his offences because "he was but a Musitian."

Marbeck wrote the first musical settings for the Prayer Book (*The Boke of Common Praier Noted,* 1550). Authorized by the Act of

Uniformity (1549), it was designed mainly for the smaller parish churches. The larger establishments had the more elaborate polyphonic settings at their disposal. It was probably not used for very long, since the revised edition, published two years later, contained polyphonic settings, preferred by choirs in the cathedrals, college chapels, and chapels royal. The first compilation of the Prayer Book was too liberal for the conservatives and too much like the Roman Catholic to suit the Reformers. The second Prayer Book was an attempt to mediate these theological differences.

The year 1560 saw publication of the first important collection of polyphonic music to appear in the Reformation period: *Certaine Notes set forthe in foure and three partes, to be sung at the Mornyng, Communion and Evenyng Praier,* etc. Its settings usually had the melody in the tenor.

Some of these early composers were especially gifted for writing polychoral music. Tallis, who was a contributor to the volume just mentioned, wrote his motet *Spem in alium nunquam habui* in forty parts, comprising ten four-part choruses. It was fairly common practice for both English and Italian writers of this period to write music for from two to twenty parts.

Early English choral music differed stylistically from that of Palestrina, in that each voice was more independent of the others. It also lacked his smoothly flowing melodic lines. Since the cathedral choirs were so small that each part often had to be carried by two voices, frequent rests were employed to permit them to catch their breath. Choral music seems to have been sung without accompaniment, at least until the time of Orlando Gibbons (late sixteenth century).

In 1587 the Rev. William Harrison described the choir's function as follows:

> In the administration of the Communion, the quier singeth the Answers, the Creed, and sundry other things appointed, but in so plaine and distinct manner that each one present may understand what they sing, everie word having but one note, though the whole harmonie consist of many parts, and those very cunninglie by the skillful in that science.[10]

By the close of the sixteenth century, the course of church music in England had been altered considerably by the influence of secular

---

[10] Winfred Douglas, *Church Music in History and Practice* (New York: Scribner's, 1937), p. 83.

30

music, especially in the use of instruments and solo work. Church music was no longer purely choral.

England's peculiar contribution to church music is the anthem, a counterpart of the motet more commonly used on the Continent. While the term is now strongly associated particularly with the development of English Reformation music, its roots go back to an earlier time. Chaucer (d. 1400) mentions the "antym" in his *Canterbury Tales*. The word itself is a perversion of *antiphon,* which over the centuries has had several meanings but in our context refers to a short scriptural passage sung before and after the Psalm or Canticle. Antiphons were very early called "anthems" in England.

The first Prayer Book contains a rubric calling for "addyng the Antheme." For the first day of Lent, the rubric "Then shal this Antheme be sayed or song" was inserted. Edward VI, however, decreed that the anthem should not be sung and the Prayer Book of Elizabeth in 1559 does not mention the anthem. Elizabeth, however, issued an injunction which provided for a special selection by the choir at the close of morning and evening prayer. The 1662 edition of the Prayer Book was the first to contain the famous rubric: "In Quires and Places where they sing, here followeth the Anthem." This referred particularly to the large churches and cathedrals where an established music program was carried on. Early anthems were unaccompanied and of a free type of composition, although later they began to take on more definite characteristics.

A number of compositions called anthems existed before 1550, but it was the middle of the sixteenth century before English composers became actively engaged in composing anthems for the Anglican service. Toward the end of the century, new forms were being developed. Thomas Morley, organist at St. Paul's Cathedral, introduced short passages for solo voice with accompaniment, as in his *Out of the Deep,* which calls for a tenor solo and a five-part choir. These experiments followed two different lines, leading eventually to the *verse* anthem and the *full* anthem. John Blow (1649-1708), organist and composer to the Chapel Royal, and Henry Purcell (1658-1695), successor to Blow at the Chapel Royal in 1682 and one of England's most eminent composers, wrote a number of the former type.

A verse anthem included solos, duets, quartets, and instrumental

31

interludes, and was not entirely unlike a cantata. Some verse anthems required up to six soloists and were sung to the accompaniment of a string orchestra, an organ, or viols. The *full* anthem was written for choir with organ accompaniment. Most of these larger works were written for the Chapel Royal, but were also performed in those cathedrals and collegiate churches that could provide the necessary musical resources.

The design of the anthem has changed little since the time of Purcell, except that the organ has replaced the instrumentalists. Purcell's verse anthem based on the text of Psalm 96 is made up as follows:

1. a long introduction by the orchestra
2. (verse 1) bass solo, with choir *alleluias*
3. (verse 2) for four solo voices
4. (verse 3) for bass solo, as before

By the early seventeenth century the verse anthem was to become the most popular by far, and most of Purcell's anthems were of this type. Not until the eighteenth century did the full anthem develop to the point where it largely replaced the verse anthem.

Not every church included the anthem in the order of worship, and its use was especially rare in the smaller churches, where choirs were hard to come by. Some churches left the anthem out on purpose, reserving its use for special church music programs. Toward the middle of the sixteenth century a number of anthems were banned because of their theology. The Royal Injunctions for Lincoln in 1548 asked that anthems about Mary and the saints not be sung, but only those about Christ as Lord of the church.

THE USE OF ORGANS

Because of the difference in opinion between the Anglicans and the Puritans on many matters relating to church affairs, church music followed a very erratic course during the first two centuries of the English Reformation. This was particularly true in the matter of using organs. In the seventeenth century they were even removed and destroyed.

Thomas Cartwright, a professor of Divinity at Cambridge University during the latter half of the sixteenth century, referred to the cathedral churches as "popish dens" and denounced both their use of organs and their singing. His violent opposition to the use of music in church eventually led to his expulsion from the university.

Sir Edward Deering, a Puritan, expressed his people's general feeling toward organs when he said that "one groan in the Spirit is worth the diapason of all the church music in the world," when he was presenting a bill for the abolition of the episcopacy.

Early in Queen Elizabeth's reign (1558-1603) there was a movement under way to remove all organs from the churches, but the bill missed being passed by one vote.

A pamphlet of 1586 states that

> the service of God is grievously abused by piping with organs, singing, ringing, and the trowling of psalms from one side of the choir to the other, with the squeaking of chanting choristers, disguised in white surplices; some in corner caps and silly copes, imitating the fashion and manner of Anti-christ the Pope.[11]

There have been periods in the history of the church when it has "been a munificent patron of art," says Erik Routley, the eminent Scottish theologian and writer on church music in our time, and there have been other times, such as the period when the Puritans were in control of the government, when "it seems to have carried restraint of art to the point of a positive cult of the ugly."[12]

The feeling against the organ subsided somewhat toward the end of the sixteenth century, but by the middle of the seventeenth century the Puritans were in power and few organs were then to be found anywhere in England.

---

[11] Edward Dickinson, *op. cit.,* pp. 370, 371.
[12] Erik Routley, *Church Music and Theology* (Philadelphia: Muhlenberg, 1959), p. 29.

III

Choir and Organ in the Seventeenth Century

THE CHOIR IN GERMANY
SECULARIZATION IN GERMAN CHORAL MUSIC

In the early seventeenth century the development of Italian opera with its arias and its orchestras had its influence on the entire gamut of church music, resulting in greater emphasis on solos as opposed to choral singing and on accompaniment as opposed to a cappella. Pure a cappella singing reached its highest point in the sixteenth century, under such masters as Palestrina and Orlando di Lasso. By J. S. Bach's time, choral selections would usually be accompanied.

Previous to the seventeenth century, music had developed almost exclusively within the bounds of church usage. Many notable composers, particularly those in Germany and England, had contributed to this development. In the seventeenth century secular forces began to usurp the position of musical leadership that churchmen had held from early times. A change was needed, obviously. As long as the development of music was hemmed in by ecclesiastical dogmas, it could not reach maturity as a form of art. Church music hereafter lost its place of preeminence in the musical world. With the performance in 1597 of Giacopo Peri's opera *Dafne,* the curtain went up on a new period in the development of music, and after Monteverdi's *Orfeo* (1607) there was no turning back. Church music was never again to be free from purely secular influences. Just as cold northerly air currents meet warm currents from the south to produce entirely new weather patterns, so the Italian opera eventually caused church music to develop such hybrid forms as the eighteenth-century cantatas and passions. The backbone of sixteenth-century German church music—chorale, motet, and early organ forms—now gave way in varying degrees to the new pressures, even though Germany had no native opera of any consequence until almost the end of the seventeenth century.

CANTATA, PASSION, AND MOTET

The cantata can be traced back to the same period that gave birth to the opera, and to the same country. Like the opera of its day, the cantata consisted of a solo part with a limited amount of accompaniment. Later in the seventeenth century it was to grow in proportions and require a larger cast of performers.

Dietrich Buxtehude (1637-1707), the Lübeck organist and composer whom J. S. Bach as a youngster walked fifty miles to hear, wrote cantata-type compositions consisting of arioso, strophic variation, ground bass, and canto-fermo treatment of the chorale. The composer-organists Georg Böhm (1661-1733) of Lüneburg and Johann Pachelbel (1653-1706) of Nuremberg wrote compositions which were not so much cantatas as variations on a chorale melody.

Stories of the Passion had been read during Holy Week from very early times. By the thirteenth century there were attempts to present the story in dramatic form. The first to write a musical setting of the Passion was the eminent Dutch composer, Jakob Obrecht (c. 1450-1505). Other composers, both Catholic and Protestant, took their cue from Obrecht's experimentation. Some of these works should rightly be called motet-passions rather than dramatic works, but the latter form soon prevailed. Johann Walther's setting of the St. Matthew Passion was the first work of its kind to be written by a German composer.

The German passion developed along rather simple lines. Employing sixteenth-century contrapuntal technique, composers continued the Obrecht motet-passion pattern, which was sung only by the choir and without accompaniment. In the seventeenth century this was re-

35

placed by passions that were conceived along the lines of an oratorio. Toward the end of the century the congregation often participated in the performance by singing chorales at given intervals.

It was in the hands of Heinrich Schütz (1585-1672) that the motet passion began to take definite form, later reaching its culmination in the monumental works of J. S. Bach. Schütz has been called "the founder of German music," and was the first to compose a real opera in the German language. But he is best known today through his church music, and in the last decade or so we have had a veritable renaissance of his choral compositions.

In his own time Schütz was best known for his passions, his *Geistliche Concerti,* and the *Symphoniae Sacrae,* the latter being regarded as his chief work. From the point of view of musical composition, Schütz stood between the old ecclesiastical style and the new monodic style and thus prepared the way for J. S. Bach. Unlike most other German composers of church music, he did not use chorale melodies or texts in his works.

It is important to know that Schütz received much of his training in Venice under Giovanni Gabrieli, an excellent Italian composer. Although immersed in a sea of Italian operatic music, Schütz managed to take what he wanted and to leave the rest alone, so that he was not submerged by the new developments in opera. Returning to Germany and his native city of Dresden, he spent the last fifty-five years of a long and fruitful life as the court chaplain of Saxony. The encouragement that the Saxon court gave to music led him to experiment with ideas he had brought back from Italy, and he wrote compositions using two or more choirs (polychoral music) and combining voices with instruments. In a number of his choral compositions he made free and very effective use of brass instruments—large groups of trombones and cornets. He probably patterned his compositions after the works of his teacher Gabrieli, who had at times included a small orchestra in his choral works and had added short instrumental interludes—a device borrowed from Italian opera.

This was not done, however, without a price. Such writing introduced the era of a more sophisticated type of church music. It was through Schütz that "concert music" made its way into the church and paved the way for the future development of the cantata, made up of arias, choruses, and instrumental accompaniment. As the concert-type of music evolved in the church, the traditional forms of the sixteenth century largely disappeared. But the unaccompanied motet and the settings of chorale melodies for choirs remained as fairly important features of church music. Some of the accompanied chorale motets of Michael Praetorius and Johann Staden also found favor, and the chorale motets of Johannes Eccard (1523-1611) were to serve as a model for the baroque period.

Schütz lived through the difficult period of the Thirty Years' War (1618-1648) and in the last years of his life found his responsibilities at the court taken over largely by Italian musicians. As in his youth, however, Schütz was not unduly influenced by his Italian colleagues, whose music was already losing its seriousness of purpose. He continued striving to give faithful representation to the more serious concepts of German art.

OTHER GERMAN CHORAL COMPOSERS

An important composer of Protestant church music in Germany at this time was Michael Praetorius (1571-1621), possibly the greatest figure in Protestant church music since the beginning of the Reformation, and certainly one of the most prolific and versatile composers of his own age. His *Musae Sioniae* contains 1,244 compositions and is a sixteen-volume set of chorale melodies with settings that range all the way from duets to quadruple choirs. The first five volumes use Latin texts, the others German. His polychoral compositions are of the earlier type that received most of its development in Venice.

While Samuel Scheidt (1587-1654) is better known today for his organ music, in his own time his choral music was more widely received. His *Cantiones Sacrae* of 1620 consisted of thirty-nine vocal compositions, fifteen of which were settings of Lutheran chorales. More will be said about him in discussing the organ music of this period.

Franz Tunder (1614-67) and Andreas Hammerschmidt (1611-75) must also be mentioned in this connection. Tunder was organist at the Marienkirche in Lübeck, a position later held by Buxtehude. Hammerschmidt was an organist and composed a number of motets, concertos, and madrigals. In his first three volumes of *Musical Devotions,* completed in 1642, he took Schütz as his model but later struck out on his own. A fourth and a fifth volume were added a few years later.

THE ORGAN IN GERMANY

THE CHORALE IN ORGAN COMPOSITIONS

Two very similar names—Schein and Scheidt—dominate the field of organ music during the first half of the seventeenth century. The problem of using the organ to accompany congregational singing has already been mentioned, and also the difficulties of having the choir assume this responsibility. The use of the latter received new impetus when Osiander began setting the chorale melody in the soprano and giving each note of the melody a separate harmonic structure.

In 1627 Johann Hermann Schein published his *Cantional,* a natural sequel to Osiander's choral music publication. Schein was then cantor at the *Thomasschule* in Leipzig, a position later to be held by J. S. Bach. Schein's chorale selections were written for four, five, or six voices, plus a figured bass accompaniment to be played by "organists, instrumentalists, and lutenists." His instructions indicate that the organist was expected to participate while the choir sang the chorale arrangement. The type of musical setting used suggests that the *Cantional* was written for use by the choir, although Rietschel [1] thinks it may also have been intended to accompany congregational singing. Rietschel, at any rate, points out that in 1637 Sigmund Stade, organist at the St. Lorenz church in Nuremberg, did accompany congregational singing with music of the type written by Schein. In his foreword to an edition of Hassler's *Kirchengesange,* Stade also mentions a similar practice, but does not state how long it had been in force.

In the works of Michael Praetorius we find similar indications. The foreword to his hymnbook of 1604 invites the congregation to join in with the choir and the organ, but apparently he expected a little less of the congregation, for he suggests that choir, congregation, and organ perform as a unit, with the choir singing the simple harmonic setting of the chorale, the organ playing the same notes, and the congregation joining in on the melody. Restricting the choir to only this type of music, he acknowledges, would put an end to the more artistic forms of choral music, which, incidentally, he did not favor.

---

[1] D. Georg Rietschel, *Die Aufgabe der Orgel im Gottesdienste bis in das 18. Jahrhundert* (Leipzig: Dürr, 1893).

Numerous references are made also to the Hamburg *Gesangbuch* of 1604, which some claim to be the first printed volume to include organ accompaniment for the chorales.

We have already considered Samuel Scheidt as a composer of choral music. We must also note his contributions as an organist and a composer for organ. Scheidt was a pupil of the renowned Dutch organist Sweelinck, and historians generally refer to him as the father of German organ music.

His *Tablatura Nova,* published 1624, consisted largely of variations on frequently used chorale melodies—one variation for each stanza—together with settings of the Kyrie, Gloria in Excelsis, etc. He gave explicit instructions here for the performance of his compositions, including the use to be made of manuals and pedals.

The *Tablatura Nova* is considered an epoch-making work in organ music because it presents a new and better treatment of the organ, as seen both from the viewpoint of the composer and of the performer. Gone were the meaningless passages that had abounded in similar publications of the past. Scheidt's figures and passages had an organic affinity with the composition as a whole, and his manner of writing for the pedals was much more advanced than that of his contemporaries.

Of the three volumes of his *Tablatura Nova* the first two contained secular pieces (for use in the home) and sacred compositions, based largely on chorale melodies, for church use. Volume III was for church use only. The structure of his sacred compositions indicates that the organ was meant to alternate with the choir, or with the clergy when there was no choir. None of this music was intended as an organ accompaniment for choral or congregational singing.

In 1650 he published his second and last work for organ, the *Tabulatur-Buch 100 geistlicher Lieder u. Psalmen D. Martini Lutheri und anderer gottseliger Männer,* which some historians call the very first chorale book to be used for accompanying congregational singing. Other writers are less specific in their claims, stating that this was the first book of its kind to come into general use.

To illustrate some of the musical styles discussed so far, here are three examples of musical composition:

1. An example of polyphonic choral music as it had developed by the early sixteenth century, taken from the 1524 edition of Johann Walther's *Gesangbüchlein:*

ERBARM DICH MEIN, O HERRE GOTT

Note that the melody is in the tenor, a characteristic of the era. Obviously the congregation would find it difficult, even disturbing, to sing along with the choir.

2. An example of Osiander's plain, straightforward harmonic setting, with the melody in the soprano:

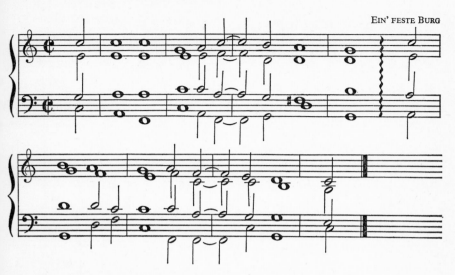

EIN' FESTE BURG

3. One of Samuel Scheidt's settings for the organ:

WACHET AUF

These three examples illustrate dramatically the transitions through which music passed from the early sixteenth century to the mid-seventeenth.

The task of arranging chorale melodies for the organ gave organists and composers a new sense of direction. Hereafter the chorale was to become inextricably intertwined with organ composition through the time of J. S. Bach. The technique of organ performers, organ music composers, and even organ builders was to be dominated by the chorale for a hundred years, and music literature would experience one of the richest chapters in its history. The chorale melodies, besides providing a natural source for the composers of organ music, were also utilized by the organists themselves. Improvisation on the chorale melodies became an aspiration of the better organists, but it also proved a pitfall for some, who began taking off on wild harmonic and melodic excursions during the congregational singing. It is interesting to note that the best organ music did not develop in Paris or Venice, where everything seemed in its favor, but rather among the poor cantors and schoolteachers of war-stricken Germany.

OTHER ORGAN COMPOSERS

The finest composers in Germany during this period—men like Pachelbel and Buxtehude—devoted their talents to developing the chorale prelude rather than freer types of music. These have stood the test of time.

Johann Pachelbel (1653-1706) was organist in Vienna 1674-77, and later at several other places in Germany, the last of which was at St. Seebald church in Nuremberg. His favorite method of treating the chorale melody was to take each phrase in the style of a fughetta, then conclude with a climactic use of the melody as a *cantus firmus*. In addition to being a prominent organist and composer in his own right, Pachelbel unwittingly transmitted the best of the Italian and South German traditions to northern Germany, where they became part of the cosmopolitan heritage of J. S. Bach, the latter being 21 years old at the time of Pachelbel's death.

Dietrich Buxtehude (1637-1707) of Lübeck has well earned his title, "father of the German organ tocatta," although he was born in Helsingör on the Denmark-Sweden frontier. His compositions based on chorale melodies are frequently fantasias, some of which are comparatively simple while others are very complex. He was well known not only for his compositions but also for the series of *Abendmusiken* (evening concerts) which he inaugurated in Lübeck—five concerts for the Sunday afternoons in Advent, which included performances by the organ, a choir, and a small orchestra. It was the fame of these concerts that led a schoolboy of Lüneburg named J. S. Bach to walk fifty miles to hear their creator perform. Not only did Buxtehude have to play for these concerts without extra remuneration, but he even had to hire what musicians he needed from the local musicians' guild.

Buxtehude's cantatas also made extensive use of orchestral instruments. His *Ihr lieben Christen freuet euch,* for example, is scored for three violins, two viols, three trombones, two trumpets, three cornets, a bassoon, and a contrabass, with an organ continuo.

ORGAN-ACCOMPANIED CONGREGATIONAL SINGING

In discussing the organ music of this era there have been a number of references to the organ's new role of accompanying congregational singing. We shall have occasion here to cite a number of orders of church worship that make specific mention of this new practice,[2] beginning with two sixteenth-century references that illustrate the role of the organ in worship previous to the more recent developments:

Brunswick (1535). For the communion service

> we see that organ, choir, and congregation have different tasks. The organ supplies a prelude, while the choir and congregation, alternating stanza by stanza, sing the complete song through. The organ then provides the transition between hymn and collect.

Strasbourg (1598). This church order permits the organ to play one stanza of the melody alone, once the congregation has sung several stanzas, after which the congregation resumes its singing. These interventions of the organ were to be so ordered as not to disrupt the thought of the text. Rietschel adds that by the close of the sixteenth century the organ was not used to accompany congregational singing.

Brunswick-Lüneberg (1657). Better than a century after the 1535 church order quoted above, we find the following:

> In the Mass it is required that after the reading of the Epistle a German psalm or chorale be sung from the hymnal. The organist may accompany these chorales.

---

[2] For these references I am indebted to Rietschel, *op. cit.,* pp. 31, 58 ff.

Note that the singing is *required,* whereas the organist *may* accompany the singing, the latter's contribution being optional rather than obligatory.

Halle (1640). In the communion service it was desirable that

the organ and any other musical instruments used should accompany (the choir) on the hymns, and the congregation should join in with them.

This statement is repeated in the Halle church order of 1660. In 1664, at the dedication of a church organ in the Liebfrauenkirche in Halle, the sermon stressed the importance of artistic music, but the program makes no mention of organ accompaniment for the hymns.

Hanau (1659). This church order allows the organist an option as to whether he shall accompany the congregation or not.

Lippe (1684). The organist is here instructed to play the songs without ornamentation, so that everyone can identify them and can sing them without difficulty.

Also revealing are some excerpts from three church orders for Mecklenburg published over a span of about 150 years:
1552. Makes no mention of an organ.

1650. Has several additions. References to the organ have to do with solo work, with no mention of accompanying the congregation.

1708. States that the organ should accompany congregational singing.

Strasbourg (1670). This church order merely repeated the instructions given in 1598 (see above) which would indicate that no changes had been made and that the organ was still not used to accompany congregational singing.

A twentieth-century German writer, Carl von Winterfeld,[3] maintains that evangelical churches which had not abolished the use of the organ altogether were using the instrument to accompany congregational singing by the first half of the seventeenth century, and that the practice was already fairly common by about 1637.

Rietschel's position seems to differ from that of Winterfeld. As evidence he cites numerous testimonials from documents of that pe-

---

[3] *Der evangelische Kirchengesang* (Leipzig: Breitkopf und Härtel, 1943).

riod, a few of which we have quoted above. His opinion is that organ accompaniment was still a rather novel practice well into the seventeenth century. Beginning about 1680 he finds a large number of church orders that mention the use of the organ to accompany congregational singing. But even in 1723, when Bach came to Leipzig, he found that the congregations there were not using the organ for this purpose. Once the organ had begun fulfilling its new role, it was also used to accompany the liturgical passages chanted by the pastor.

ORGAN-BUILDING

Many of Germany's fine organs were ruined during the Thirty Years' War (1618-48), when progress in organ-building came to a halt. Many of the royal chapels were closed, their musical organizations were disbanded, and their long tradition of systematic musical instruction was broken off.

After the war the Lutherans began in earnest to provide organs for their churches. Privately owned organs were often donated to the poorer congregations, and many a community raised funds to buy a new instrument for the local church. Organ dedications became gala events, and visitors came to them from great distances. In those days the regular church organist was often an amateur musician from the community, for the war had disrupted many an organist's education.

For several years after the close of the war the church was the only agency supplying music to the community. The royal courts spent many years restoring their choirs and orchestras, and only a few people benefited from these, anyway.

Among the special features of seventeenth-century organ building was the increase in the amount of gadgetry. Not only could the organist roll the drums and crash the cymbals—he could pull a nightingale stop; he could imitate a cuckoo or a bumblebee or the bleating of a goat. He could even activate the morning star or the sun, and as a special attraction for Ascension Day he could pull a picture of Christ to the ceiling of the church, to the accompaniment of trombone and lute stops!

CONCERT MUSIC

After the organ had become well established in its new role in the church service, there was a tendency to introduce other instruments as well, the introduction of which began to transform worship services

45

into "sacred concerts." The choir now dwindled in importance as the organ and other instruments gained prominence.

When J. S. Bach was a choir boy at St. Michel's in Lüneberg (1700), the church there maintained a well-balanced program of choral and instrumental music. A complete choir and orchestra performed on a number of the feast days, and also on other occasions. In addition to anthems and spiritual arias there were motets, hymns sung in parts, and concerted church compositions.

In 1633 the orchestra and organ played for chorales sung by the Danzig congregation. In some other places the orchestra accompanied the choir and the organ played for the congregational singing.

Hermann Schein of Leipzig (d. 1630) was the first to introduce the "spiritual concert" into the liturgy. In a number of places this was to become the chief musical part of the service. Heinrich Schütz (d. 1672) relegated the chorale to a secondary position, as is shown in his *Opella Nova,* the first such work to contain the so-called *concerti ecclesiastici.* Instruments such as harps, lutes, trombones, cornets, violins, and flutes were now regularly found in the larger churches.

If the schedule of the organist at Cittau in 1639 can be taken as a sample, we might well conclude that organists of that period had little opportunity to become bored with their leisure time, especially if we figure in the hours they must have spent practicing. The Cittau organist was expected to be in the church at 5:30 A.M. on Sundays, in order to play the organ for the students' choir, which sang the *Te Deum Laudamus* while the organist accompanied on a small instrument near the high altar. At 7:00 A.M. in the summer (7:30 A.M. in winter) he played the big organ for these services. At 2:00 P.M. he played for a second service. This was the schedule for holidays as well, and on the eve of full-dress services a vesper service required his presence. He also played for weddings, which were scheduled for 11:00 A.M. The only respite the organist could look forward to was the period from Invocavit Sunday to Good Friday, the Advent season, and a few other designated occasions when the organ was not used.

DECLINE IN CHURCH MUSIC

Several factors were to contribute to a decline in church music that set in toward the end of the seventeenth century, but it can be attributed in part to the influence of Italian opera music. Once the dramatic recitatives, arias, and choruses had become standard fare for operatic

46

composers, they began serving as models for church music composition. The simple congregational singing that had been encouraged by the early Lutheran reformers was now relegated to a secondary position in the service. The sturdy chorale gave way to oratorios, cantatas, and passions performed in a theatrical fashion.

The improvement of orchestration was a part of the operatic development, and this too was pressed into service in the cause of church music. Instrumental music now became more important than choral music. The office of cantor, the *Kantorei,* and the church choir were in many cases eliminated. Often the organist was the only church musician, and even he, as a rule, possessed neither liturgical nor technical training. Whereas the choir had been an essential feature of the sixteenth-century service, it now gradually lost all its importance. There was also an economic factor: it cost considerably more to maintain a choir than an organist.

A second factor contributing to the decline in church music was the devastating Thirty Years' War, which began as a series of quarrels between the Catholic and Protestant princes of Germany but eventually involved several other countries, including Denmark and Sweden. Before the Peace of Westphalia finally concluded this struggle, Germany and other European nations found themselves exhausted and depleted of their resources.

A third factor was the advent of pietism, a movement that stressed the practical and emotional aspects of Christianity and depreciated its doctrinal and ecclesiological aspects. The influence of pietistic ideals caused a decline of interest in theology and the arts, and churchmen who aligned themselves with this movement had little interest in church music. The central figure of German pietism was Philipp Jakob Spener (1635-1705), who preached at Strasbourg and Frankfort and became court preacher at Dresden in 1686.

CHOIR AND ORGAN IN SCANDINAVIA
GERMAN MUSICIANS IN SWEDEN

In the seventeenth century the German Protestant musical tradition was transplanted to Sweden. Georg Weber, a German who had settled in Stockholm, published his *Geistliche Lieder* in 1640. Another German, Andreas Düben, became court organist in addition to his duties as organist for the German church in Stockholm. Düben's home became a center for such musical activities as choral and orchestral performances and organ recitals. Gustav, his Swedish-born son, who eventually replaced his father at court and in the German church, was a good friend of the Lübeck organists, Tunder and Buxtehude. He was also an eminent performer; he composed pieces for choir and instruments, and he used his standing in music circles to attract a number of visiting composers and performers to the Swedish capital.

Among the German publications more widely used in Sweden before the end of the seventeenth century was Cruger's *Praxis pietatis melica* (published in Germany about 1644) and Scheidt's *Tabulatur-Buch* of 1650.

ORGANS AND ORGANISTS

The organ did not figure very prominently in Swedish church music during most of the seventeenth century, largely because organs were too expensive. Some organs were built in Sweden, others were imported from Germany. There were some of considerable antiquity: *Storkyrkan* in Stockholm, installed an organ in 1680, replacing a 1498 instrument; Linkoping Cathedral, installed one in 1619; Visby Cathedral, 1600; the German church in Stockholm, 1590; Uppsala Cathedral, about 1680. By the close of the century, organ-building and organ performance in this remote country had reached a high point.

The Swedish organist's duty was to intone the vocal parts of the service, to support the choir, to alternate with it, to play solo passages; he also alternated with the congregation on the chorales and occasionally even played short independent selections. The function of the Swedish organist had from early times been more important than that of the cantor, who led the choral music.

Before the century was over, Sweden had its own official chorale book, the *Koralpsalmboken* of 1697, which the organist could use to accompany congregational singing. Old and new melodies had been collected, and old songs were given a new musical setting, which included figured bass. With the advent of this book, the organ became a popular instrument for accompanying congregational singing.

Koralpsalmboken was prepared by Olof Rudbeck and Harold Vallerius, the latter being director of the Stockholm University music department. The book was well received and continued in use until the early nineteenth century.

But the Rudbeck-Vallerius publication was also a signal for the organists to begin taking over the musical elements of the service. In numerous instances choral and congregational music suffered because the organist was monopolizing the singers' time. They had to be counseled not to perform merely for the purpose of displaying their technique and not to play music that was inappropriate for worship.

The tendency toward secularization in German music also became a factor in Scandinavia. Pietism also moved in, although somewhat later than in Germany.

CHOIRS IN SWEDEN

The Swedes developed considerable interest in choral work during the early seventeenth century. Both choir and congregation contributed to the singing of the service, but the choir was more prominent in the early part of the century—when the congregation sang only a few familiar hymns—whereas congregational singing had grown more important than choir music by the end of the century.

Part music was taught in the schools, and wide use was made of contemporary German music, including compositions by Eccard, Vulpius, Praetorius, and Schein.

In the middle of the century, Bishop Laurellii's directive to the churches asked that

> in all congregations, especially in the cities, one should endeavor to sing the fine congregational songs in such a manner that the choir and the rest of the congregation are always in agreement, and with tone neither too loud nor slow, or too hasty. In towns the schoolchildren should be urged to sing in the choir. In the rural areas where no choir singing is possible, the precentor when leading the singing should stand in the middle of the church to keep the simple and unlearned group singing correctly.[4]

The precentor commonly enlisted the aid of some wind or string instrument, such as the violin or the clarinet.

THE SITUATION IN DENMARK-NORWAY

Reference has already been made to the fact that Sweden got its first Lutheran hymnal in 1526. Norway and Denmark (who at this period were subject to the same ruler) got theirs in 1569—forty-three years later. Sweden's first chorale book for the organist was issued in 1679, whereas the first chorale book for Norway-Denmark appeared in 1764—sixty-seven years later.

---

[4] Preben Nodermann, *Studier i Svensk Hymnologi* (Lund: Sydsvenska Bok- och Musikförlaget, 1911), p. 114.

In other words, Norway-Denmark lagged considerably behind Sweden, partly because of what was happening to these countries politically. These three Scandinavian countries were involved in wars intermittently over the centuries. Sweden was frequently victorious in her wars, while Norway and Denmark met as often with defeat. Denmark, for instance, was involved in the Thirty Years' War from 1624 to 1634, during which time she was humiliated, but Sweden, who entered the war later (1630-36), emerged victorious. There were subsequent skirmishes among the northern powers, from which Sweden gained additional territory from both Norway and Denmark by the time the Peace of Roskilde was signed in 1658. All of this made Sweden the unquestioned leader of the Nordic nations.

The bibliography that concludes this present volume lists four sources published in Norway and six in Denmark. Four of the ten volumes are on music in general and the remaining six deal with church music in particular. But in all ten volumes there were almost no references to choirs or organs for the period we are now considering.

Danish and Norwegian churches had a few choirs and organs during the early Reformation period, but very few organs were added to the list in the seventeenth century. In Frederiksborg one of the most unique organs in Denmark is still in use today. It was built in 1610 and was presented by the Landgrave of Hesse to Christian IV of Denmark. It was installed in 1617 in the Royal Church at Frederiksborg, just north of Copenhagen. In 1692 it was moved to the Royal Knight's Hall but by the close of the eighteenth century it was back in the church. In 1895 it was taken to the Frederiksborg court and completely restored. The organ has two manuals of 45 keys each and a pedalboard. All the pipes are of wood and of the finest workmanship. You might well expect an organ built in the early 17th century to sound like a "chest of whistles," but its tone bears a marked resemblance to that of present-day instruments.

The *klokker* (cantor) was at this time undoubtedly the outstanding musical figure on the Danish-Norwegian scene. The office of *Klokker,* instituted about the middle of the sixteenth century, had for its main responsibility the leading of congregational singing. An important publication of this period was Kingo's *Gradual* of 1699, which contained the hymn tunes then commonly used.

CHOIR AND ORGAN IN SWITZERLAND

Neither Calvin nor Zwingli, the two leading Swiss Reformers, looked with favor upon the use of choir or organ in the church service, and their attitude was bound to have an adverse effect on church music in their respective spheres of influence. Calvin even felt that instrumental music was tolerated in the Old Testament era because the people of God "were then in infancy." As for using organs in churches, this was much too reminiscent of "popery," which was one thing he wanted to avoid at all costs.

Calvin died in 1564, and it was a hundred years before a few Swiss churches began installing organs, the cost of these being met in some cases by the government and in others through some kind of fund-raising plan. Organs continued to be a rarity in the rural churches, however.

Vocal music in this era was for the most part restricted to congregational singing of metrical versions of the Psalms, sometimes sung in unison, sometimes in four-part harmony. Congregational singing of part-music often presented considerable difficulties, but it was through such a medium that the Reformed churches of Switzerland preserved this genre of church music. In 1606 a Basel organist published a complete musical setting of the Psalter, the first Swiss composition to put the melody in the soprano. But four-part congregational singing was not actually practiced in Basel until the eighteenth century. The favorite settings for the Psalms at this time were the simple versions of Claude Goudimel, a French composer who had taken up his abode in Geneva.

The seventeenth century also saw the establishment in the larger population centers of *collegia musica,* amateur choral organizations that did not confine themselves to singing in church. Their repertory, however, included four-part settings of the Psalms, and the participation of church members in the practice sessions was bound to increase their singing skill, which in turn tended to raise the level of congregational singing.

Selections from the Goudimel Psalter were sung during the church service proper, and other religious selections were sung after the conclusion of the service, a kind of counterpart to the postludal organ recitals given in Dutch churches.

In Basel the four-part psalter was sung, and the organ was used to accompany the singing, but Bern used wind instruments for accompaniment. In the Engadine a paid singing organization was employed, and their repertoire consisted of more intricate pieces of music, including some compositions of the Dutch composer Sweelinck. But the Engadine was an exception to the general rule.

CHOIR AND ORGAN IN SCOTLAND

In 1638 the General Assembly of the Established Church of Scotland openly registered its opposition to the use of organs in public worship, even though King Charles would have preferred to have organs in the cathedrals and larger churches, since one was then being used in the Chapel Royal. But the Directory of Worship, adopted in 1645 and effective until late in the nineteenth century, made no provision for the use of organs.

Samuel Rutherford, a Scottish preacher educated at Edinburgh University, stated in his *Divine Right of Church Government* that he had no liking for the "droning of organs." And Charles Mouat commented that "musical instruments are not to be used in God's worship." [5] These statements should suffice to illustrate that church organ music was not very popular at the time.

Choral music did not fare much better. The use of part music was officially recognized in 1625, after it had already been used for a while in the Chapel Royal. Some of the Scotch strictness toward the use of part music was relaxed early in the seventeenth century, when the Episcopal movement in England first struck Scotland. Since part music was being employed in the Anglican services, many of the Scots were fascinated by the contrast between this and their own simple psalmody. The more conservative Presbyterians, of course, still condemned this as being too "popish" a practice.

In 1617 the Chapel Royal adopted the English service, which included the use of organ and surpliced choir. It was also Anglican influence that led in 1625 (or even sooner) to the publication of four-part settings of the psalter. By 1621 we find evidence that a special body of singers was being used in worship, although this was not necessarily a choir that sang part music. They may well have been a small group of students who assisted the precentor in the psalm-

---

[5] Henry George Farmer, *op. cit.*, p. 207.

singing. References are made to the "singing master and his bairns" sitting together and leading the congregation in song.

Until at least 1625 there were no choirs in the Church of Scotland. Where there was singing at all, it was done by the congregation and not by a choir, except in the Chapel Royal, which was a law unto itself.

In 1635 Edward Millar published a setting of the psalter for four voices, done in more of a contrapuntal style instead of the plain note-against-note harmony. Some have called this the greatest of all Scottish psalters. It seems to have been designed for choirs that stood in rows facing each other, since the right-hand pages were printed upside down.

It is unlikely, however, that Millar's Psalter was ever used in church, so that its publication should not be considered a harbinger of musical growth. In fact, Charles I was trying so hard to force Episcopalianism on Scotland that the Scotch people began reacting against everything English, including part-singing, which was associated with the English style of church music. The reaction had grown into open revolt by 1657. Musicless psalters now appeared, and it is thought that simple psalm-singing by the congregation may even have disappeared for a time.

The Authorized Version of the Psalter, published 1650, not only contained no tunes but gave no suggestions as to how the Psalms were to be sung. The glorious period of the Scottish Psalter had come to an inglorious close. The precentors, whose duty it had been to lead congregational singing, now had nowhere to turn. For 150 years they were to be left without instructions or aids in their work.

The official attitude taken by the Church of Scotland was thus a very negative approach, and only feeble efforts were made by anyone to promote choral singing. Only by the second half of the eighteenth century would the situation begin to improve.

CHOIR AND ORGAN IN ENGLAND
PURITANISM

The seventeenth century was a most difficult period for any kind of church music in England. The Puritans gained the upper hand in government and in 1644 mustered enough votes to pass a bill that would retard the growth of church music in England for many years to come.

As early as the reign of Queen Elizabeth an effort was made to remove all organs from the churches. The measure was defeated by only one vote. By the early 17th century a musicless ceremony had largely replaced the English Choral Eucharist, which was not to be fully restored until the nineteenth century.

It was not that the Puritans had no liking for music. Many Puritans were fine performers of vocal or instrumental music. Oliver Cromwell, for instance, owned an organ, employed an organist, and held choral music in high regard. He also engaged an orchestra to play at his daughter's wedding. The Puritan poet John Milton was also an organist.

The following quotation aptly describes the situation at that time:

> the doom of the medieval organs was not due to any Puritan objection to music; rather it was to their proper dislike of the somewhat frivolous style of playing and singing that had grown up in the early part of the seventeenth century, both in and outside the churches.[6]

The same author quotes a Mr. Prynne as saying in 1633 that

> musicke now-a-days has growne to such and so great licentiousness that even at the ministration of the Holy Sacrament all kinds of wanton and lewde trifling, with piping of Organs have their place and course. As for the Divine Service and Common-prayer it is so chaunted and misused and mangled that it may justly seeme not to be a noyse made of men, but rather a bleating of bruite beasts.

The climax of the Puritans' revolt against music in the church came in 1644, when they succeeded in passing a bill through the two houses of Parliament that attacked the use of any kind of art in the churches.

Again quoting Canon MacDermott:

> The Lords and Commons assembled in Parliament, the better to accomplish the blessed Reformation so happily begun, and to remove offences and things illegal in the worship of God, do ordaine that all representations of the Trinity, or of an Angell or Saint in or about Any Cathedrall, Collegiate, or Parish Church or Chappell or in any open place within this Kingdom shall be taken away, defaced and utterly destroyed . . . and that all Organs and the frames and cases wherein they stand in all Churches and Chappells aforesaid shall be taken away, and utterly defaced, and none other hereafter set up in their places.[7]

---

[6] Canon K. H. MacDermott, *The Old Church Gallery Minstrels* (London: SPCK, 1948), p. 3.
[7] *Ibid.*, p. 2.

Some organs seem to have escaped this treatment by their removal to homes, inns, or other places. The organs in St. Paul's Cathedral, York Cathedral, Lincoln Cathedral, and Christ's College were not removed. Thus, despite the radicality of this Act of Parliament, not all the organs were wantonly removed and destroyed. But it is safe to assume that they were silenced for a time.

Not only were the organs silenced but choir books were also burned. The cathedral service was abolished, and the singers were told to seek some other occupation "not so offensive to God."

When the Puritan law was passed, many English parish churches had organs, despite all the opposition to their use over the years. Of course there were many people, even in the reign of Henry VIII, that felt he should have gone a bit further in his reformation and banned "curious singing" and instrumental music. As early as 1536, organ playing had been listed as one of the "84 Faults and Abuses of Religion." At that time a number of bishops and archbishops were opposed to its use in church, and there were even some organs removed.

In 1619 George Wither, a Puritan, complained in *A Preparation to the Psalter* that many organists were taking too much liberty and that they ran on "too fantastically in their voluntaries." Perhaps the organists themselves were largely to blame for the Puritan reaction, and one must also consider that very little respectable or appropriate music was being written for the organ.

Because the elimination of music from the service made it impossible to follow the liturgy of the *Book of Common Prayer,* the Puritans replaced the Prayer Book with their *Directory for Public Worship of God in Three Kingdoms.*

THE RESTORATION

When Charles II became king of England after sixteen years of Puritan rule, there were very few organs left in his domains, but those that survived were refurbished and put into use. The Prayer Book liturgy was also reestablished.

Charles, during his exile on the Continent, had become fond of the lighter music of the French, who had progressed farther in secular music than the English. After the coronation, Charles sent Pelham Humfrey, a member of the Royal Chapel Choir, to study music in Paris under the renowned Jean Baptiste Lully. When Humfrey returned to England, he was appointed "Composer in Ordinary for the Violins to His Majesty." Following the precepts of his able teacher, Humfrey introduced the use of violins to accompany the anthem, which now included solos and long instrumental interludes. Because this was the kind of music King Charles preferred, it was the kind that Humfrey composed and performed. The older polyphonic music, used by court choirs of yesteryear, was now discarded. The effects of Charles II's innovation can be traced even to our own day.

The older composers had difficulty writing to suit the new monarch's taste, but the younger ones were more successful. In 1662, for example, John Evelyn, an attendant at the Chapel Royal, wrote in his diary:

> One of His Majesty's Chaplains preach'd, after which, instead of ye antient, grave and solemn wind musiq accompanying ye organ, was introduc'd a concert of 24 violins between every pause, after ye French fantastical light way, better suiting a tavern, or a play-house, than a church. This was ye first time of change, and now we no more hear the cornet which gave life to ye organ; that instrument quite left off, in which the English were so skilfull.[8]

In addition to restoring the use of the organ and the liturgy, it became necessary also to reedit the *Book of Common Prayer*. Edward Lowe, a professor of music at Oxford University, was assigned this task. His *A Short Direction for the Performance of Cathedrall Service* was published in 1661.

Church music did not fare very well under Charles II, since, as we mentioned earlier, the Stuarts had little personal regard for music in general and even less for music in the church. In many areas the money allocated for church music was brazenly siphoned off for other uses. Choirs, left to their fate, often deteriorated completely. At St. Paul's, for example, where there had normally been a thirty-voice choir, only six singers were retained. And a number of the clergy showed no more interest in church music than did Charles himself.

The following commentary on organs and choirs was published in 1642, two years before the Puritans issued the decree banning their use:

---

[8] John S. Bumpus, *op. cit.*, pp. 124, 125. The "cornet" mentioned was a wooden instrument used at Westminster Abbey to support the choir when needed.

THE ORGAN'S FAREWELL, OR THE QUERISTER'S LAMENTATION

We may now abjure our singing
For ceremonies bringing
Into the Church, and ringing
    For the downfall of the Organs.
    Alas! poor Organs.

A Querister may hang himself
For wanting his diviner pelfe;
    He's ta'en now for a clergy elfe:
    Alas! fond Superstition.

Let Ceremonies then deplore
Their fortune, greater than before:
    Down, Idols, Crosses, Ceremonies!
    Alas! poor Ceremonies.[9]

REESTABLISHING THE ORGAN

For about two centuries following the 1644 ban on organs, they were found only in a few (and the very largest) English churches. The cathedrals began installing organs again shortly after the Restoration, but most of the small village churches were without organs until the latter half of the nineteenth century. One exception was the tiny All Saints Church in Hertford, which installed an organ in 1698.

Organ-building had come to a standstill under the Puritans, when a number of builders left the country to continue their trade elsewhere. One of these was Thomas Harris, who went to France but returned after the Restoration to continue his work. A number of foreigners were also invited to England to help reestablish this highly skilled trade. Among these was Bernard Schmidt, who came from Germany. He was appointed "Organ Builder in Ordinary" to Charles II, and worked with Thomas Harris in introducing new ideas from the Continent. The organs they built were not equipped with pedals because there was so little demand for them. But the manuals were capable of producing 16-foot tones.

In 1700, Henry Dodwell published in London a book entitled *A Treatise Concerning the Lawfulness of Instrumental Musick in Holy*

---

[9] Sydney H. Nicholson, *Quires and Places Where They Sing* (London: SPCK, 1932), pp. 43, 44.

Offices. This title indicates the mood of his day. Dodwell was of course in favor of instrumental music in the church, especially the organ. The preface to this small volume, which is about as long as the book itself, was written by F. Newte. Among the arguments advanced by those who are opposed to music, Newte lists:

1. That the use of organs in Christian assemblies for divine worship is condemned as unlawful by the Book of Homilies.
2. That if the praising of God with organs be thus lawful in the worship of God, then will it for the same reason be lawful to introduce other musical instruments in the worship of God, as harps, trumpets, etc.

Some people also felt that instrumental music in worship would lead to other ancient practices, as circumcision, bloody sacrifices, and dancing to instrumental music.

Dodwell's volume was occasioned by a sermon preached at a recent organ dedication, which had as its title: *Concerning the Lawfulness and Use of Organs in the Christian Church.* An unknown writer criticized the speaker at the dedication as "Jewish and popish and inconsistent with gospel worship." Dodwell's volume was the third phase of this skirmish—a reply to the critic. Dodwell asks

> Have they [our adversaries] any express testimonies of the New Testament that musical instruments in the service of God are unlawful, sufficient to countervail the notoriety of fact, avowedly practis'd to the contrary? [10]

THE GALLERY MINSTRELS

Since the Puritans during their ascendancy had disposed of almost all the organs, and since it took quite a few years to reestablish organ-building, it was necessary in the meantime to use the Psalms and Canticles as spoken responses in the order of worship or to sing them without accompaniment. When Charles II advocated the use of instruments in the Chapel at Whitehall, he seems to have given a signal to all the churches to begin using instruments. This ushered in a rather curious age of church music known as the "Gallery Musicians" era. It was characteristic of the rural and smaller churches, beginning about 1660 and lasting in some locales for a couple of centuries.

---

[10] Henry Dodwell, *A Treatise Concerning the Lawfulness of Instrumental Musick in Holy Offices* (London: William Haws, 1700), p. 4.

The gallery musicians were groups of from three to eight instrumentalists, usually half strings and half woodwinds, and occasionally a brass instrument or two. The musicians were usually self-taught and musically illiterate, but so devoted to their task that they practiced several times a week. Some were so proficient that they could play more than one instrument.

The singers who worked with them also took pride in their work. One choir would claim it was the best in the area, another that it had some of the best singers, a third that it could sing louder than any other! Only uncouth amateurs could have indulged in such gross rivalries as these bands of gallery musicians.

The following excerpts from writings of the period will help give a pew's-eye view of these musicians:

It is sad to hear what whining, yelling and screeching there is in many congregations, as if the people were affrighted or distracted.

The singing was almost ludicrous . . . provoking laughter rather than expressing praise. . . .

The screeming treble of the children and the rude bass of the men were agonizing to his sensitive ears.

The more shrill-toned they . . . may be, the more valued they are.[11]

The demeanor of these groups was often quite unceremonious, as the following will illustrate:

A certain Mr. Brown was choirmaster, and the parish clerk, who sat in state in his black gown at the bottom of the "three-decker," bore the sweet-sounding name of Larkaby. When the parson got to the end of the third Collect, Mr. Larkaby would stand up and put the question to the bandmaster in the gallery, with his hand to his mouth to make it more impressive.

"Any singing to-day, Mr. Brown?" The latter would turn round and look at his band, and reply "No, Mr. Larkaby, bain't hands enough"; or, if there were six or seven players, "Yes, Mr. Larkaby!" Then the clerk would turn his eyes towards the parson in the reading-desk above him and say, "You can goo on!" and a psalm or hymn would be given out and sung.[12]

---

[11] Canon K. H. MacDermott, *op. cit.,* p. 9.
[12] *Ibid.,* p. 6.

The clergy seemed little interested in what these bizarre choirs did, and lent them little assistance—but at times they voiced their criticisms.

In the Devon area, a group of about a dozen boys and girls constituted the choir, assisted by a violin, a cornet, a trombone, and sometimes a clarinet and a flute. For the first part of the service they sat secluded in the west gallery behind curtains. When the hymn was to be sung, the curtains were noisily drawn open and the congregation turned around in their pews, back to the altar, and literally "faced the music."

> From his box below the pulpit William Clogg, the parish clerk, gave out the hymn with the usual preface: "Let us zeng to the praäse and glary of Goad." Then, might be heard from the Gallery the word "pitch!" and the sound of a tuning-fork struck by the choir-leader, with the remark, "Doänt'ee zeng till I do zeng!" He marked the time of the hymn by stumping all through with his wooden leg. The artificial limb was also used as an instrument of correction on the boys of the choir, and the girls were rapped with the tuning-fork; sometimes the harmony was interrupted by the yell of a sufferer. Meanwhile, the good Richard Clarke [the director] offered admonitions which could be heard all over the church. "Zeng oop, zeng oop, or I'll whack'ee I'ull. Zeng oop, there's visitors in rectory pew." [13]

The band in this particular church was active until replaced by the harmonium in 1868.

One might be charitable enough to excuse (if not even condone) the carryings-on of the gallery minstrels. They were a dedicated lot and for the most part sincere. Not only did many of them practice more than once a week, but they laboriously copied out the music needed by the group. They were on their own, financially, and some members were so dedicated that it was not uncommon to find people who had been active in the group for forty to fifty years. Attending a church service with such a band in the gallery, the worshiper upon hearing them begin to play would

> do as the other members of the congregation do—turn round to the west with your face to the gallery and your back to the altar. . . . You need not try to join in the singing unless you wish; leave the music to those who are deft in the art, they will more gladly forgive your silence than your attempt to sing.[14]

---

[13] Sydney H. Nicholson, *op. cit.,* pp. 56, 57.
[14] Canon K. H. MacDermott, *op. cit.,* p. 1.

To conclude this presentation, the following is quoted from Canon MacDermott's interview with a Sussex "musicianer" (or "musicker," as these people were called) which he included in his volume on the gallery minstrels:

No, there warn't no organ in them days. Don't suppose we ever had one in the old church; we had a band, up in the gallery over the big door. Rickety old stairs up to it and dark, too. Let's see, there was Jim Comber, the Clurk, he played the flewte; Steve, the cobbler, he played clar'net, and old Tomsett, 'Grimy Tom' we called him, he were a blacksmith, he scraped away on the gran'mother fiddle, the bass-viol, y' know. An' they *could* play too; tarrible fine playin' 'twas, I reckon. I was on'y a little chap at the time, over eighty year ago, and me and my brother Tom were allowed to sit in the gallery 'cos we could sing. Us boys sung seconds and if we didn't just sing out, Old Jim 'ud crack us over the head wi' his flewte. There wur two or three fiddles, too, and a horse's leg—that's what we called the bassoon. We sat up in the gallery and I used to count the winders doorin' the sarmon, whilst Cobbler wiped his clar'net dry wi' a big red han'kerchief, and the Smith he tooned his big fiddle. No, the passon didn't mind 'bout that; he jest kep' on a-preachin' and preachin', and when he'd done one hour he wiped his spartacles and turned the hour-glass tother way up and went on agin. Tarrible long sarmons in them days, they was! No, there warn't many books then; the clurk he had a printed book and the singers and minstrels wrote their own books. Here's one my feyther used, writ all by hisself. Yes, good writin' 'tis, they knew how to write then, as well as sing. Which is the melerdy? Oh! the *air* you mean; there 'tis. Yes, the tenor allus sung the air, not the trebles; us boys on'y sung seconds as I was a-telling on ye afore. An' when we sung out too loud, the men they glared at us and told us we was a grout-headed set o' chaps. Hymn-books? No, we didn't have no hymns; leastways, on'y the Marnin' Hymn and one for Easter and Chris'mas Day. We sung the Old Varsion of the Psalms, or sometimes the Noo Varsion, any on 'em we liked and anywhen we liked, too. No, vicar, he didn't care what we sung and told us to bawl out what we pleased, s'longs we didn't bother him! [15]

THE BARREL ORGAN

It was during this period of the gallery musicians that other types of music were introduced into Reformation worship. One of these was the barrel organ, usually a portable instrument, operated by turning a crank and pumping the bellows. This instrument was generally used where no gallery band existed.

---

[15] *Ibid.*, pp. 5, 6. This interview was held in about 1898.

Barrel organs were built as early as 1598 and were still being manufactured as late as the mid-nineteenth century. Some of these had more than one stop, some had none. They were usually supplied with three revolving wood "barrels," or cylinders, each having from ten to twelve tunes. They were about 42 inches long, 8 to 9 inches in diameter, and set with pegs that opened the appropriate valves on the organ in such a pattern as to play a tune. The instruments had a limited number of pipes, just enough to play in two or three keys.

Some barrel organs existed as more than museum pieces well into the twentieth century. In the early 1900's a fine specimen belonging to an Essex church was disposed of quite unceremoniously. The pipes were sold to a journeyman tinker, the bellows to the village blacksmith. The boards in the air chests became a bed for an aged man, and the case of the instrument was converted into a pigsty!

Many of these instruments escaped such a fate. Some, in fact, are still in playable condition. Others have been incorporated into pipe organs or converted into "finger organs" (with a keyboard). Peter Philips, an English organist and composer, arranged a madrigal for the barrel organ and Handel wrote several compositions for it.

Some of the cylinders available contained both religious and secular tunes, which could lead at times to embarrassing situations, such as the occasion when the barrel organ in a Sussex church failed to stop at the proper time, and the congregation was regaled with a comic song entitled "Little Drops of Brandy" after having played the proper hymn. As if this were not enough, it gave another "click" and continued with "Go to the devil and wash yourself!"

THE ENGLISH CHOIRS

For churches favored with "regular" choirs instead of gallery minstrels, there were good collections of choral music on the market again by the early 1660's, and John Playford's famous *Introduction to the Skill of Music* was a great aid in reviving choral societies. Another helpful publication, published in 1663, was *The Divine Services and Anthems Usually Sung in the Cathedrals and Collegiate Choirs of the Church of England,* which listed over 400 recommended anthems.

Since the churches had not been training boys to sing during the Puritan period, this program had to be started again from scratch. Some composers wrote for choruses of men's voices, others used "cornets" to carry the treble parts, all of which helped to fill the gap until boys' voices could again be used to take the treble parts in worship music.

Two prominent composers of the period were Pelham Humfrey, already mentioned, and Henry Purcell (1658-95), who was organist at Westminster Abbey from 1680. Both Humfrey and Purcell were court composers.

Even though the publisher Novello issued six volumes of *Purcell's Sacred Music,* and despite the fact that Purcell is one of England's all-time greats as a composer, we have to realize that his impact on church music has been rather slight, because he failed to give it the profound expression it needs for use in worship. This becomes all the more evident when we compare his church music with that of Heinrich Schütz in Germany, who died when Purcell was a lad of fourteen years. Purcell's contribution to music in general was of enduring value, but church music was not his strong point.

Purcell's death in 1695 (at the age of 37) brought to its close a glorious age of English music that had begun with John Dunstable, when Western music was in its artistic infancy. Two centuries were to pass before England could again boast of native composers, in church music or otherwise, who could hold their own with composers on the Continent. Even today the works of English church music composers are practically unknown to musicians on the Continent.

Before the seventeenth century came to a close, musical activities in the larger churches were again well organized. Much had been accomplished since February 28, 1664, when Samuel Pepys, himself a fine amateur musician, wrote in his famous *Diary:*

> Up and walked to St. Paul's. But before and after sermon I was impatiently troubled at the Quire—the worst that ever I heard.[16]

Whereas the seventeenth century of church music in England had begun on a dismal note, by its end there was at least one choir director who had developed an enviable tradition of good morale and proper working conditions for his musical organization. Here is how Henry Aldrich, Dean of Christ Church in Oxford, managed his choral affairs:

> First, He never admitted a Boy Chorister, unless he had been previously instructed, and had given sufficient Proof of his Abilities: By

---

[16] Sir Frederick Bridge, *Samuel Pepys, Lover of Musique* (London: Smith, Elder, 1903), p. 92.

this Means, he had always a complete Set, and a constant Supply: For Parents seeing that such Children who had Merit, were certain of being preferred as Opportunity offered, were very solicitous to get them instructed in Readiness. In admitting a Sing Man or Chaplain, he made it a Rule to give Preference to one who had merited his Favour in a lower Capacity; provided nevertheless he was properly qualified when he was a Candidate for either of these Places. By a strict Observance of this Method, there was not an useless Member in his Choir; for Chaplains had then an equal share of Choral duty with the Singing Men; nor was there the least Grumbling or Complaint on that Account.[17]

To show that even good choirs have their weaker moments, we append this note by Dr. Cyril Jackson, director of the same choir about a century later:

A boy with no more ear than a stone, nor no more voice than an ass would be an excellent chorister.[18]

By the middle of the nineteenth century, this same choir had the reputation of being the worst in all of England.

CHOIR AND ORGAN IN THE NETHERLANDS

The Dutch practice, begun in the sixteenth century, of having the organist play postservice and sometimes preservice recitals, was continued into the seventeenth. Constantin Huygens (1596-1687), Dutch patriot and author, also secretary to Prince Henry, wrote critically of the use of the organ in the Dutch Reformed church of his day:

At the conclusion of the sermon, the prayer, and the closing song we allow the organ to be played. The tune is that of the Psalm which was sung last. I ask: what is the use of that noise? What influence do those wordless tones have on our dispositions? It is said: We come fresh from the holy exercises, and our ears are filled with them as we leave. . . . But let us be honest. The two hours which we necessarily have spent in the church in a sitting position have so wearied us, so sated us with seriousness, that we are glad to be dismissed, and we long for some news, the streets, the sky. It is certain that of one hundred church members, not one is found who pays the least attention to the organ. . . .

Meanwhile, the Psalm is ended in a light mood, its three or four verses poured into all manners of art, bent into all kind of swings. And, if the

[17] John S. Bumpus, *History of English Cathedral Music* 1549-1889 (London: T. Werner Laurie, 1908), p. 183.
[18] *Ibid.*, p. 184.

organist is not inclined to start a second one, he follows up with his dreams: well-meant; madrigals, as they are called, of all kinds, according to the books. At last a postlude, just the same as the prelude, to which only the janitor and a few cripples listen. So the unedifying noise stops.[19]

It must be kept in mind that throughout this period the organ and organist were under the supervision of the town council and not that of the church. Ecclesiastical resistance to using the organ *in* the service was gradually weakening, however. The Synod of Edam in 1586 concluded that every church in possession of an organ should consult the local authorities as to how to make the best use of the instrument. The 1638 Synod of Delft went farther and stated that organ-playing was hereafter to be a neutral subject and its use in the service was to be left to the discretion of the local churches.

The first move to integrate the organ with the Dutch Reformed service came in 1636. Following a series of meetings between church and city officials, it was agreed to allow the use of the organ *during* the church service. A detailed statement on the use of the organ, published in 1640 by Huygens, is still used by the Dutch Reformed Church at the present time.

Obviously one could not expect that after a century of debate over the use of the organ it would be accepted universally all at once. Some churches refused for another two centuries to have organs, and there are still churches of Dutch Reformed origin in the United States that share this feeling.

It is ironical that Jan Sweelinck (1562-1621), possibly the greatest of all Dutch organists and an active member of the Dutch Reformed Church, should have to live and labor in a time when Dutch churchmen were most hotly debating the use of his instrument. After studying with Gabrieli in Venice, Sweelinck came to Amsterdam as organist and remained in this capacity from 1580 until his death. It was he who made of the choral prelude a separate composition, developing it out of his extemporizations on chorale melodies—a technique that J. S. Bach would later bring to maturity. His style of composition was more indigenous to the organ than that of any contemporary composer in Italy, England, or France.

Since the early fifteenth century Dutch composers had been recog-

---

[19] Henry A. Bruinsma, "The Organ Controversy in the Netherlands Reformation to 1640," *Journal of the American Musicological Society*, VII (1954) pp. 210-11.

nized as leaders in choral composition. Men like Guillaume Dufay, born about 1400, and Johannes Okeghem, born around 1430, did much to establish this reputation. But greatest of the fifteenth-century composers was Josquin Deprès, a student of Okeghem, whose music was to be of absorbing interest to Martin Luther. Orlando Lasso, born in Belgium about 1530 and a student in Italy until 1555, finally settled down in the Netherlands and is now claimed by that country as one of its great composers. Sweelinck also, in addition to his achievements in organ composition, wrote choral motets. Since choirs were not used in church services during his era, his compositions were not intended for liturgical use.

While the Dutch Reformed Church had its beginnings in the late sixteenth century, conditions were very unsettled for quite a while, due among other things to the Arminian controversy in theology, which lasted until about 1619. With all this infighting going on, there was no time for choral music in the Dutch Reformed Church, and the superb technique of Lasso was all but forgotten by the middle of the seventeenth century.

IV

The Century of Johann Sebastian Bach

IN GERMANY

THE PRE-BACH PERIOD (TO 1703)

Tremendous forces were unleashed in the world of music during the late 17th and early 18th centuries. Sixteenth-century polyphonic techniques had culminated in the incomparable works of Palestrina. Now the stage was being set for another climactic breakthrough: the harmonic-contrapuntal technique of J. S. Bach. We have already noticed that the influence of seventeenth-century opera and instrumental music had done much to alter the church's choral repertoire. The "sacred concert" concept, introduced into church music by Heinrich Schütz, continued to be prominent in the works of subsequent composers. Instrumental music was coming into its own, but it would be another century before the orchestra would become a complete performing medium in its own right.

Protestant composers employed *concertato*-style instrumental music in their settings of the chorale melodies, which meant using a blend of voices and instruments. Works written for solo voices and orchestra could now be used in place of the motet before the sermon, and the transition was accomplished without a breath of opposition, one reason being that the town council had more to say about church music activities than the congregation.

Another innovation indicative of the unsettled conditions was the introduction of female voices into a few choirs here and there. Johann

Mattheson, Hamburg Cathedral cantor 1715-28, is generally credited with this change. He used three or four women in his choir, against stiff protests at first, but with growing favor as the people became more accustomed to the practice. Nevertheless we cannot say that his experiment was either widespread or long-lived.

Pietism, a fact to be reckoned with in the seventeenth century, became even more deeply ingrained by the first half of the eighteenth. It is difficult to imagine that such competent and respectable composers as Georg Philipp Telemann (1681-1767) and Reinhard Keiser (1673-1739) could have given their passions such titles as *Blissful Reflection upon the Sufferings and Death of Our Lord,* or *The Bloody and Dying Jesus.* Considering that pietism did not look with favor on art of any kind, there was little that church music could do but deteriorate.

Johann Kuhnau (1660-1722) lived in a time when there were attempts to bring opera and church music closer together. Kuhnau, Bach's immediate predecessor at the Thomasschule in Leipzig, tried to unite the accompanied church music of the previous century with the opera-influenced church music of the eighteenth century. His cantatas, while not of the dramatic type, were not based on the chorale, either.

Hamburg in the early eighteenth century produced such composers as Telemann (already mentioned) and George Frederick Handel (1685-1759). Both of these men wrote numerous operas and also some church music, or—more correctly—music for the church. Their goal actually was to introduce "religious opera" into the church services, because they considered this a more genuinely "Protestant" type of church music. Lutheran composers for the most part were wary of writing Biblical operas. Composers like Kuhnau had been basically opposed to this operatic type of music for church purposes, and yet they allowed themselves to be influenced by it. By the early eighteenth century even a number of the clergy were in favor of this theatrical type of music, maintaining that it represented an ancient ideal of church drama. Eventually this led to adopting "secular" texts, not unlike those found in Italian operas. Since most of the music was in the form of solo work (arias or recitatives) the choir as such had less opportunity to perform.

Into this chaotic situation stepped Johann Sebastian Bach. Had he followed the trend of the times he would have gone down in history as only another of the illustrious Bachs, many of whom were great musicians. That he had his own sense of values and charted his own course must be attributed to his firm religious convictions. Bach was undoubtedly familiar with church music practices in Hamburg, for he had made frequent trips there to hear the great Jan Reinken, organist at St. Katherine's for over a half century and renowned for his skill in improvising. But Georg Böhm, Bach's teacher in Lüneburg, and Buxtehude in nearby Lübeck were the models whom Bach was to follow in preference to the Hamburg musicians. Böhm used the chorale melody extensively in his organ compositions, amplifying and decorating it while providing support with a simple harmonic accompaniment over a *basso ostinato*—the repetition of a characteristic figure in the pedal. Buxtehude did much the same.

By the time Bach reached maturity he had at his command all the elements necessary for musical composition and production. The cantata and passion had gained their full stature; the chorale prelude and fugue had taken definite shape; the organ was a highly refined instrument, and organ performance in Germany was of a very high order.

THE BACH PERIOD (1703-50) AND ITS HERITAGE

Bach and the Organ

In 1702 Bach was graduated from the St. Michael's school in Lüneburg, at the age of seventeen. The following year he received his first professional appointment, the New Church in Arnstadt, where he had at his disposal a recently renovated and enlarged organ. It was a two-manual instrument with twenty-one ranks of pipes for the manuals and five for the pedals. As organist and choir director he made the most of his opportunity to continue the development of his organ technique and was soon distinguishing himself as a superb organist.

After four years at Arnstadt, Bach spent one year at the St. Blasius church in Mühlhausen, followed in turn by two court appointments: the court of Duke Wilhelm Ernst in Weimar (1708-17) and that of Prince Leopold of Anhalt-Cöthen (1717-23).

In Weimar he was chapel organist and chamber musician, with no responsibilities for choral work. The Duke may unwittingly have contributed to Bach's development as a composer by making available to him his immense library of Italian music. Bach found the smoothly flowing melodic lines of these Italian composers quite different from the more involved and angular melodies of north German composers.

69

It was at Weimar that Bach composed his Toccata and Fugue in D Minor, his Passacaglia and Fugue in C Minor, and a number of other great works.

Bach's position at Cöthen does not seem to have suited him so well. Prince Leopold's church orientation was Reformed rather than Lutheran, whereas Bach and his family attended the orthodox Lutheran church. The court organ was also rather small, although he may have had access to a larger organ at the Reformed church in town.

These situations appear not to have hampered his activities as a composer, however. During his years at the Cöthen court he composed his Two- and Three-Part Inventions, the celebrated Fantasia and Fugue in G Minor, numerous chorale preludes, cantatas, and many other works.

Bach's next—and last—position was at the Thomasschule in Leipzig, where he undertook his duties in 1723, at age thirty-eight. As his career had begun in a church, so it was to end in one. Many of his important compositions came from this latter period, when he emphasized choral music more than he had before.

Bach's interest in a school position must have been prompted in part by his concern for the education of his children. It was not so much that he considered himself an academician, for he lacked university training, had had no experience in formal classroom work, and could boast no scholarly writings to his credit. The committee responsible for engaging a teacher would have known of him as an organ virtuoso, but this would have had little bearing on their decision. Several of Bach's contemporaries, now largely forgotten, were first considered for the position, and at that time would have been preferred for it.

In addition to his teaching duties at the Thomasschule, Bach also had the responsibility of supplying music for four Leipzig churches: St. Thomas, St. Nicholas, the New Church, and St. Peter's. St. Thomas and St. Nicholas each had four-hour services starting at seven in the morning, and their schedule ran as follows:

Organ Prelude—during which the choir gathered in the gallery
Motet—by the choir, in Latin
Introit—by either a Catholic or Lutheran composer
Kyrie—sung in both Latin and German
Gloria—intoned from the altar to which either the choir responded

with *et in terra pax,* or the congregation with *Allein Gott in der Höh, sei Ehr.*
Collect
Epistle—read or sung
Hymn—by the congregation
Gospel
Credo
Cantata—after the organist had played a prelude in the various keys needed for tuning the instruments in the orchestra. The organ accompanied the choir and orchestra with a *basso continuo.*
Hymn—*Wir glauben all an einen Gott*
Sermon—one hour in length
Prayer
Blessing
Hymn—by the congregation
Communion Service—during which hymns were sung

Nor was this four-hour service the end of the day's activities! Another service followed at noon, and there was a two-hour vesper service at one-thirty.

It will be noted that the motet was sung in Latin. Since Bach did not write motets with Latin texts, one would assume from this that he used works by other composers. Like the cantatas, these were sung to the accompaniment of organ and orchestra.

The cantor usually left the church after the cantata, and his duties for the remainder of the service were handled by a student assistant. Bach, however, was probably in the habit of staying for the communion service, which gave him an opportunity to play preludes and improvise on communion-hymn melodies.

As an organist, Bach was recognized as supreme. How unbounded would have been his enthusiasm if the resources of some of today's organs could have been his to command! He would have had to revise his pedal technique, of course, since the pedals in his time were quite short and did not require much use of the heels. Schweitzer, the eminent Bach biographer, said this about Bach's pedaling:

> In pedaling, Bach could not use the heel because the pedals of his day were so short; he had to produce every note with the point of the foot. Moreover, the shortness of the pedals hindered the moving of one foot over the other. He was, therefore, often obliged to let his foot glide from one pedal on to its neighbor, whereas we can manage a better legato than was possible for him by moving one foot over the other, or by using foot and heel alternately.

When I was young I found the short pedal of the Bach period still existing in many old village organs. In Holland many pedals are even today so short that to use the heel is impossible.[1]

As an organ performer, Bach's biographer Forkel wrote in 1803,

When John Seb. Bach seated himself at the organ when there was no divine service . . . he used to choose some subject and to execute it in all the various forms of organ composition so that the subject constantly remained his material, even if he had played, without intermission, for two hours or more. First, he used this theme for a prelude and a fugue, with the full organ. Then he showed his art of using the stops for a trio, a quartet, etc., always upon the same subject. Afterwards followed a chorale, the melody of which was playfully surrounded in the most diversified manner by the original subject, in three or four parts. Finally, the conclusion was made by a fugue, with the full organ, in which either another treatment only of the first subject predominated, or one or, according to its nature, two others were mixed with it. This is the art which old Reinken, at Hamburg, considered as being already lost in his time, but which, as he afterwards found, not only lived in John Sebastian Bach, but had attained through him the highest degree of perfection.[2]

Bach's playing and his compositions are written in a kind of Gothic style, as though he were out of step even with his own times, and so he was. Most church musicians of his day were taken up with all sorts of artificialities and gimmicks, but these are not to be found in the majestic music of Bach, which is in fact so dense and complex that it cannot be easily grasped in a single hearing. As Schweitzer says,

In Bach's music, much more than in that of any other composer, the plastic outline of the whole is the result of the optical effect of the details; it requires, in order to become visible, a synthetic activity of the hearer's aesthetic imagination. Even to the best musician, at a first hearing, a Bach fugue seems chaos; while even to the ordinary musician this chaos becomes clear after repeated hearings, when the great lucid lines come out.[3]

Because Bach, besides being a top-flight organist, also understood the inner workings of the instrument, he was frequently called upon to test new organ installations. He would begin his examination by drawing out every stop and playing with full organ to determine "whether

---

[1] Percy A. Scholes, *Oxford Companion to Music* (London: Oxford, 1950), p. 663.
[2] Hans T. David and Arthur Mendel, *The Bach Reader* (New York: W. W. Norton, 1945), pp. 315, 316.
[3] Albert Schweitzer, *J. S. Bach*, trans. Ernest Newmann (2 vols., New York: Macmillan, 1923), I, 213.

the organ had good lungs." Many of the instruments he tested were probably better organs than his own in Leipzig. Organ dedications in those days were great events, attracting huge audiences from wide areas, and these gave the composer-organist an opportunity to display both his ingenuity as a composer and his skill as a performer. When complimented on a performance, Bach once replied:

> There is nothing remarkable about it. All one has to do is hit the right notes at the right time, and the instrument plays itself.[4]

The organs in Bach's time were about as completely equipped as those today, but seventeenth- and eighteenth-century custom seemed to dictate the use of only one stop per part. When the performer felt the need of varying the tone, he usually added stops at a different pitch instead of combining stops on the same pitch.

Bach's original organ compositions actually contain very few instructions for performing them. Only in a few instances were notations made as to the length of pipes—four-foot, eight-foot, or sixteen-foot—or an occasional indication of the manual to be used.

At the time of Bach the Palestrina type of pure vocal polyphony had become almost nonexistent. The choir sang to the accompaniment of an organ or of an organ and instruments, and the smallness of the choirs and their general lack of ability made this accompaniment almost a necessity. Johnn Kuhnau, Bach's predecessor in Leipzig, had used the harpsichord to accompany the choir, but it seems unlikely that Bach did this except for rehearsals and perhaps for a few performances that called for additional instrumental support.

Spitta says concerning Bach's time that "in Leipzig, as everywhere else, it was the custom to accompany the motet on the organ or some other supporting instrument." [5] According to Spitta there is still extant a figured organ part that Bach wrote for his motet, *Der Geist hilft unsrer Schwachheit auf.*

It was after the time of Bach that unaccompanied singing was introduced at Leipzig—perhaps under J. F. Doles, who was cantor 1756-89. Spitta mentions that in 1767 the organist-composer Ernst L. Gerber heard the Thomasschule choir sing a motet without accompaniment "as was their custom at that time." It is hard to say whether

---

[4] David and Mendel, *op. cit.,* p. 313.
[5] Johann August Spitta, *Johann Sebastian Bach* (3 vols, New York: Dover, 1951), II, 607.

Bach would have preferred his own motets sung without accompaniment if conditions in his day had favored this kind of performance.

We have already noted that the organ was being used in some churches to accompany congregational singing before the middle of the seventeenth century but that this was not the practice as yet in Leipzig, and would not be until the eighteenth century.

The 1709 Church Order of Braunschweig-Lüneburg instructed the organist to play through the hymn once, then to accompany the congregation softly so as not to overpower them. The foreword of the Wernigeroder hymnal of 1712 makes no mention of the organ's being used there for this purpose, but the pastor is instructed to sing with the choir so that the congregation will be further assisted in keeping the right tempo. One hundred years later the church in Wernigerode had begun using the organ for congregational singing.

In Nordhausen, however, the organist still played one stanza alone and a postludium, but did not accompany the singing. The 1735 edition of their hymnal mentions that the organist had a chorale book, which would indicate that by this time he was in the habit of accompanying congregational singing. A more definite statement is made in the 1747 Church Order of Ulm, to the effect that the organ is of great help in congregational singing, especially in the larger churches. During Lent, however, the organ was not used at all in the regular service. A prelude was played for the Communion Service, and at its close the organ joined the congregation in *Gott sei gelobet*.

A letter written 1770 by the organist Buttstett and preserved in the public records of Rotenburg informs us that a full 20 years after Bach's death this city was still using church orders it had formulated in 1611 and 1668. Neither of these made any provision for organ-accompanied congregational singing. Even in the late nineteenth century the East Frisian churches (and some in other areas) still maintained the custom of alternating the singing and the organ-playing on successive verses.

Bach and the Choir

In none of the positions that Bach held does he seem to have enjoyed conditions favorable to good choral work. At the New Church in Arnstadt—his first position—it was customary for the three churches of that city to obtain their singers from the *Gymnasium*. This meant not only that his singers were generally lacking in talent but that they were rather unruly as well, and Bach was no disciplinarian—nor even a teacher, for that matter. Rehearsals must have been a time of excruciating discomfort to the 18-year-old cantor!

His position at St. Blasius church in Mühlhausen seemed attractive at the outset because of its competent and dedicated choir. But difficulties arose when the avowedly pietistic pastor, Johann Frohne, insisted on dictating most of the congregation's musical policies, as he had in the past. Theologically, Bach found himself more in harmony with the orthodox element of Lutheranism, which made his position untenable. He left after only one year.

While Bach was at the court of Duke Wilhelm Ernst in Weimar, he became interested in a church position at Halle that carried with it considerable prestige. For an appraisal of his qualifications, Bach wrote a cantata that placed him at the top of the list of applicants. But when he learned that the salary would be less than he was getting at Weimar, he declined the appointment. This incident, however, marked the beginning for Bach of a sustained drive to compose cantatas, of which he had previously written very few. At the Thomasschule a few years later he would compose cantatas by the score. Bach's early cantatas show a stronger Italian influence in their free employment of the aria, whereas his later cantatas are more distinctly characterized by his use of the chorale.

Bach's interest in the Halle church position involves a paradox not adequately explained by the circumstances, since his reputation as an organist should have enabled him to secure any church position he really wanted. Perhaps he preferred to remain at court because of his especially agreeable relations with Duke Wilhelm, which suffered no serious setback until the death of Kapellmeister Johann Samuel Drese in 1716. When Bach was not appointed Kapellmeister to fill this vacancy, his disappointment led him to think of leaving, despite all the personal interest the Duke had shown in his work and the numerous promotions and salary increases he had received. Conditions became critical when Bach was drawn into a quarrel between the Duke and the Duke's nephew.

Before being released from his Weimar duties, Bach had accepted an appointment with Prince Leopold of Anhalt-Cöthen and had received money from him to move his family and personal belongings. The Duke's refusal to release Bach threw him into a violent rage, which the Duke undertook to cool off by throwing him in jail. Court records reveal that Bach spent over three weeks in confinement, and upon release was given notice of an unfavorable discharge.

When Bach came to the Thomasschule in Leipzig, he had at his disposal a choral society of fifty-four men and boys, subdivided into four choirs that supplied music respectively for St. Thomas, St. Nicholas, the New Church, and St. Peter's. Since ten to twelve of these singers were simultaneously members of the orchestra, each of the four choirs averaged less than a dozen singers. Subtracting from this number the inevitable absences due to illness and allowing further for the limited vocal capacity of some of the boys, one can see that Bach was confronted with the same sort of limitations that beset most church choirs. The minimum requirement for each of the first three above-named churches was that there be three singers on each of the four parts; in St. Peter's it was two to a part. The younger and poorer singers were used in the St. Peter's choir because chorales were the only music required there. Each of the four choirs sang the simpler music under the direction of a student assistant, with Bach himself conducting the more intricate compositions. He accomplished this by dividing his time between St. Thomas and St. Nicholas churches, with student leaders replacing him in his absence from either place.

Bach's orchestra consisted generally of six violins, two violas, two cellos, a string bass, two or three oboes, one or two bassoons, and some flutes and trumpets—a total of about 18-20 performers. Eight of these were town musicians supplied by the city council; Bach had to complete his instrumentation by drafting school choir members. The orchestra, as you can see, was always larger in numbers than the choir it accompanied, a proportion apparently dictated by contemporary custom. Under Bach and Handel the vocal-instrumental balance was reversed, and by mid-century the choir customarily had more members than the orchestra.

On high festival days there were both morning and afternoon performances of accompanied music at St. Nicholas and St. Thomas. Bach was at one church in the morning, his assistant at the other; in the afternoon the two choirs exchanged places, each performing the same music it had sung in the morning.

Cantatas were sung every Sunday except during Lent and the last three Sundays in Advent, seasons when the organ was also not used. The choir had additional responsibilities on these special occasions:

They sang the Nicene Creed (in Latin) and led the congregation in the singing of the Litany after the Epistle. Cantatas were also required on 59 special feast days each year: New Year's Day, Epiphany, Ascension, etc. Bach reportedly composed five complete sets of cantatas for the church year—a total of 295—only 190 of which we know anything about. Some of the treble arias in the cantatas would probably have been too difficult for the immature voices of the boys, but it was customary to use adult falsetto voices for these.

It was still a prevailing practice to use Latin texts with the motets sung in church services, but none of Bach's motets were based on the Latin texts, because he did not intend them to be used by the smaller church choirs but by the entire Thomasschule choral ensemble, which was large enough to handle the double-choir movements that most of these compositions contained.

Bach's passions, on the other hand, were written for use in the church service. The first performance of his *St. Matthew Passion,* given at St. Thomas on Good Friday of the year 1729, required the use of two choirs, two orchestras, and an organ. His orchestras on this occasion numbered from forty to forty-five members, and the total number of singers, including soloists, was not over thirty-two. Bach is said to have conducted this performance from a clavichord, with an assistant at the organ to give the chords for the recitatives. The congregation probably joined in singing the chorales.

Bach's *Mass in B Minor* was written for a court function and was therefore not intended as church music. His initial purpose was to write only the first two movements, but these proved to be major works in their own right. When the entire *Mass* was finished, its immense proportions rendered it unsuitable for use in a church service.

We know little about Bach as a choral director, but we do know he was not a good organizer and often had difficulty managing his ill-mannered boys. Sometimes the rector had to be called in to establish order. The city council frequently held Bach responsible for these difficulties, and Bach for his part was often annoyed by actions that the council took.

We do not know exactly how Bach directed his group, but the common practice of conductors in his time was to use a rolled-up sheet of music paper and to do the directing from whatever instrument the conductor normally used. Some directors played the violin and could come quickly to the aid of any ailing part. From 1730 on, it became more common for the conductor to be at the harpsichord.

A letter by Johann Matthias Gesner gives us some estimation of Bach in action as a conductor:

> . . . watching over everything and bringing back to the rhythm and the beat, one of thirty or even forty musicians, the one with a nod, another by tapping with the foot, and a third with a warning finger, giving the right note to one from the top of his voice, to another from the bottom, and to a third from the middle of it—all alone, in the midst of the greatest din made by the participants, and, although he is executing the most difficult parts himself, noticing at once whenever and wherever a mistake occurs, holding everyone together, taking precautions everywhere, and repairing any unsteadiness, full of rhythm in every part of his body—this one man taking in all these harmonies with his keen ear and emitting with his voice alone the tone of all the voices.[6]

Taking this statement at face value it is evident that the singers in his group were not very reliable, supporting the observation that by Bach's time there was a dearth of true vocal art in Germany, even in the schools. As further evidence of this we have Bach's own notations on his choir boys. He records that a certain boy is "somewhat wanting in accuracy of ear" or that "in singing he is not skilled," and so on. It is obvious from all his recorded remarks on this subject that he speaks as a musician and not as a singing master. He never alludes to how the voice is used, to evenness of register, or to other vocal technicalities. All he looked for in a singer was that he have a good sense of pitch, be accurate in keeping time, and, if possible, possess a pleasing quality of voice.

The deficiencies of the singers were probably an important factor in his liberal use of instrumental accompaniment. The practice of combining cornets and trombones with the choir had become rather common even in the seventeenth century, and was well established in Leipzig by Bach's time. The motet was generally accompanied by the organ, and during those seasons when the organ was not used, the choir did not sing a motet.

We have noted previously that Bach was out of step with his own time, an age dominated by pietist theology whose influence was espe-

---

[6] David and Mendel, *op. cit.*, p. 231.

cially heavy in the area of art and church music. Bach tried to maintain the traditions of an already disappearing technique, and it is fortunate for posterity that he did so. With his passing there was no one of sufficient stature or motivation to continue his works. In fact, church music was becoming decadent long before Bach died.

The Rehabilitation of Bach

The death of Johann Sebastian Bach in 1750 marked the beginning of the end for a noble musical family that for generations had been prominent in many parts of Germany. Some of his sons were the last of the Bach family to win a place in the annals of music history.

His death also marked the end of an era for music in general and church music in particular. The cantorate choirs became rapidly extinct. Volunteer choirs were started in some communities but were not permitted to sing in church. The groups that survived were at too low a level musically to cope with the intricacies of a Bach cantata, and the orthodox texts that went with these works did not appeal to pietistic tastes. Church music outside the church, notably that of Bach's illustrious contemporary, George Frederick Handel, now began to flourish.

It remained for a twenty-year-old Lutheran Jew—Felix Mendelssohn—to revive interest in the works of J. S. Bach seventy years after the latter's death, when most of Bach's choral works had been buried in oblivion. In 1829 Mendelssohn conducted Bach's *St. Matthew Passion* in Berlin, using the *Singakademie* chorus and an orchestra comprised of personnel from the Philharmonic Society and the Royal Band. Mendelssohn conducted while seated at the piano. This performance was enthusiastically received, both for its superbly written music and the excellence of its execution. Mendelssohn's sister Fanny described the reactions of those rehearsing for the performance in a letter to a friend:

> The people were astonished, stared, admired; and when, after a few weeks, the rehearsals in the academy itself [where it was to be performed] commenced, their faces became *very* long, with surprise at the existence of such a work, about which they, the members of the Berlin Academy, knew nothing.[7]

Enthusiasm for the work spread so quickly by word of mouth that by the night of the first performance people were standing in line to be

[7] Percy M. Young, *The Choral Tradition* (London: Hutchinson, 1962), p. 138.

admitted, and the hall was filled in fifteen minutes. A second performance was given ten days later, again to a capacity crowd. Additional performances were given in Breslau and Königsberg shortly thereafter, and in 1841 Mendelssohn conducted a performance in Leipzig.

Other Bach enthusiasts also made their influence felt. Schelble, the founder of the Frankfort *Caecilienverein,* performed parts of the *B Minor Mass* in 1828 and in 1831. Johann Mosewius (d. 1858) an opera singer and writer, published as well as performed the works of Bach. He especially promoted the churchly qualities of Bach's music, although in this he had to stand alone against the majority, who felt that much of Bach's music was theatrical and dramatic.

The revival of Bach's choral works thus came about under circumstances quite different from those for which they were written. Originally intended for church worship, they were now given as concert productions. This meant, of course, that the larger works were the ones usually performed. His cantatas, which required an orchestra, were not published, but his motets were not only printed but were performed regularly in Leipzig. Of the five Passions written by Bach, only *St. Matthew* and *St. John* are now extant. Because so little of Bach's music was published in his lifetime, it was not until the twentieth century that the full impact of Bach's greatness struck the musical world. The organization of the *Bachgesellschaft* in 1850 provided the first systematic plan for publishing his works, the final volume of which appeared in 1900. That same year saw the organization in Leipzig of the New Bach Society, whose objective was to restore Bach's music to its rightful place.

Many of Bach's works were first prepared for publication by well-meaning but not authentically informed editors. Many of the Romantic Age editors were so influenced by their own times as to add tempo and dynamic indications that did violence to Bach's own conception of how the compositions were to be performed. A lot of printer's ink has been used to indicate crescendos, diminuendos, and even swells that were never a part of Bach's music.

THE POST-BACH ERA

As we have mentioned, a decline in church music had set in long before Bach's death. This was to continue throughout the latter half of the eighteenth century. Numerous accessories had been added to the organ during the pre-Bach century, but the true state of church music is sized up by Dr. Charles Burney, an English music historian who visited the Continent in 1770. He comments concerning a large church organ built 1722 in Germany, which had over 3,000 pipes:

> At each wing [of eagles as if in flight, mounted at the doors] is a kettle drum, which is beat by an angel placed behind it, whose motion the organist regulates by pedal; at the top of the pyramid, or middle column of pipes, there are two figures, representing Fame, spreading their wings, when the drums are beat, and raising them as high as the top of the pyramid; each of these figures sounds a trumpet, and then takes its flight.

> There are likewise two suns, which move to the sound of cymbals, and the wind obliges them to cross the clouds; during which time, two eagles take their flight, as naturally as if they were alive.[8]

Other organs had crowing roosters which flapped their wings; cuckoos, nightingales, and other birds sang songs. An organ in Ochsenhausen was equipped (appropriate to its name) with an ox that sang like a cuckoo. Some organs had a bumblebee to awaken sleepers for the offering. By pulling the "star stop," some organists could set in motion a gilded sun with gleaming rays, driven by the shaft of a windmill blown by the bellows mechanism of the organ.

Dr. Burney also recorded his impressions of a visit to the Lutheran *Frauen Kirche* in Dresden, where

> there is a projection for the Communion table, over which is placed a most magnificent organ. This is the only instance I can recollect, of an organ being placed at the *east* end of the church. I had hitherto only seen it at the west window, at the west end of the choir, or on one side.

> The singing here, with so fine an instrument, has a very striking effect. The whole congregation, consisting of near three thousand persons, sing in unison, melodies almost as slow as those used in our parish churches; but the people being better musicians here than with us, and accustomed from their infancy to sing the chief part of the service, were better in tune, and formed one of the grandest choruses I ever heard.[9]

On Sundays and festival days, Burney says, the choir from the school sang cantatas: "the most noble I have ever heard." The organ in this church was one of the most celebrated of its time, having been built by

---

[8] Percy A. Scholes, *Dr. Burney's Musical Tours in Europe* (London: Oxford, 1959), p. 165.
[9] *Ibid.*, p. 140.

the famous Silbermann of Neuburg. It had forty-eight stops, of which seven were reeds, and a two-octave pedalboard.

Some churches curtailed the use of organs in the second half of the eighteenth century. Cantors were dismissed from their posts and many choirs had to be disbanded because the church and city authorities had reduced their financial support. The practice of training choirs in the schools very nearly disappeared. When in 1789 Johann Adam Hiller assumed the role of cantor at Thomasschule, he felt it was practically impossible to carry on Bach's practice of providing musical assistance to the churches of Leipzig.

Instrumental music now reigned supreme in the church service. Most of the larger choral works—oratorios, passions, cantatas—were no longer being composed for the church service but to be performed as dramatic productions. Karl Heinrich Graun's celebrated *Der Tod Jesu,* the most famous passion of the eighteenth century, was first performed in a theatre.

The church musician's post was now usually occupied by paid secular musicians, who not infrequently held simultaneous positions in Protestant and Catholic churches.

Thus we may say that Protestant church music declined rapidly in Germany during the half-century following Bach's death, and its recovery was to come very slowly indeed.

IN SCANDINAVIA

THE ORGAN: GERMAN INFLUENCE AND EARLY CHORALE BOOKS

Organs were becoming somewhat common in Denmark in the eighteenth century. Whereas a number of handwritten chorale books were already in use, the first printed work of this type was the *Fuldstaendig Koral-Bog,* published in 1764 by F. C. Breitendich, who served as organist at the Royal Court and at Nicolai Kirke in Copenhagen. It contained chorale melodies with a figured-bass notation.

The first chorale book with full notation to be published for Denmark and Norway was prepared by Niels Schiørring and published in 1781. Schiørring had studied in Germany with a son of Johann Sebastian Bach. In fact, the preface of his volume states that Carl P. E. Bach has examined the work very carefully.

Organs were not very numerous in eighteenth-century Norway. The organ now in Trondheim Cathedral was built by a Dutch firm in 1741. The Vor Frelsers organ in Oslo dates from 1729 and was probably Dutch-built also. The Bergen cathedral organ is of 1749 vintage.

Sweden and Finland had 495 organs between them in 1773, and during the early eighteenth century a number of prominent organ builders were active in Sweden. The first Swedish chorale book was *Koralpsalmboken,* published 1697, whose musical notation utilized the figured-bass system. The first chorale book to have all four parts written out—Georg Vogler's *Koralbok*—was published in 1798, a whole century later. And this volume was not authorized for use in church.

Evidently the eighteenth-century Scandinavians had no universally established musical traditions of their own. Trained musicians came from elsewhere, notably Germany, or Scandinavian musicians went elsewhere to study. Sweden was making more rapid progress in this direction than Norway and Denmark, with the possible exception of Copenhagen, which was becoming something of a musical center.

The musical language of the Scandinavians, therefore, resembled that of northern Germany; only the technical terms were different. The German organists plagued worshipers by inserting *Zwischenspiel* (interludes) between the stanzas of a hymn; the Scandinavian organists did the same thing but called it *Mellemspilene.* The only other difference was that the Scandinavians, who lacked a certain measure of the German skill and know-how, were not able to add quite as many embellishments. But the Scandinavians were not beyond using questionable music for their worship services. A booklet published in Norway about the middle of the nineteenth century complains about organists who play "wretched marches" or waltzes at the close of the service in order to display their "childish vanity" and cleverness. All this made many people wish there were no organ in the church at all.

In late eighteenth-century Scandinavia, as in Germany of the same period, Rationalism affected church music as much as it did theology.

It is interesting to note that plans were made in 1795 to subject all Swedish organists to an examination that would determine their professional qualifications. The proposal failed, however, for lack of support. The plan, as set forth, would have made a distinction between the higher- and lower-paid positions. Those aspiring to better positions were expected to play general bass accompaniments with chords in the left hand and the melody in the right and also with chords in both hands. They must play preludes in all the keys, based on a given theme, and they must play preludes and fugues, both in the older fugal style and in more contemporary idioms. In the smaller communities the organist was also expected to be proficient on his instrument, but should also be able to play the violin by note at dances, to accompany on the cello, and to have some proficiency on a wind instrument.

This type of examination proposal was premature at the time, but today it is common practice in much of Protestant Europe.

THE SCANDINAVIAN CHOIR CRISIS

Whereas choirs were a prominent feature of Swedish church music in the seventeenth century, their use diminished as congregational singing gained in importance. There must have been some use of choirs during the eighteenth century, however, since there is extant a complaint—just after the turn of the century—about the slow tempo used in the hymn singing, which is attributed to an earlier use of the choir to accompany congregational singing. Yet it is safe to say that choral work in eighteenth-century Swedish churches was negligible and that the Danes and Norwegians had even less. Many of Sweden's best-trained church musicians left their posts early in the eighteenth century, to the detriment not only of organ music but of choral and congregational singing as well.

REFORMED CHURCH MUSIC
DESUETUDE OF THE ORGAN

When Dr. Charles Burney, the English music historian, toured Europe in 1770 he noted that two Geneva churches had organs and that they were used only for psalmody "in the true purity of John Calvin." Actually there is very little we can say about Swiss organ music in this era. Although the cathedral in Bern had an organ by mid-eighteenth century, and Zürich had its first organ by the second half of the nineteenth century, the reintroduction of organs to Protestant Switzerland was in general a very slow process.

In Scotland the Reformed congregations were unavoidably influenced by Anglicanism after the 1707 Act of Union that brought Scotland and England under a common ruler. The Reformed churches were adamantly opposed to organs and choirs in worship during the early part of the century, and congregational singing of the psalms had all but disappeared. The Episcopal churches of Scotland, though small and financially embarrassed, were in possession of organs, choirs, and a certain amount of good music.

The first organ to be played in Scotland was probably the one installed in the Episcopal Chapel at Aberdeen in 1730. Edinburgh's Episcopal Chapel had an organ by 1747, and an excerpt from a Newcastle journal of 1757 records that a number of organs were being shipped to Scotland:

> By a master of the ship just arrived at Shields we are assured that seven fine organs are gone from London to Edinburgh . . . two of which are for the city, the other five for west-country kirks.[10]

These organs, obviously, were for Episcopalian and not Scotch Presbyterian churches. The issue of having organs in the Presbyterian churches of Scotland was to become hotly controversial in the nineteenth century, as we shall see later.

The organ received about the same treatment in the Dutch Reformed Church as it had in Switzerland. The Dutch, however, had never completely forbidden its use, thanks to the influence of the town councils. The fact that the Dutch Reformed Church permitted the liturgical use of the organ before the mid-seventeenth century would indicate that Netherlands congregations were far ahead of Switzerland and Scotland in this respect. Dr. Burney also visited Amsterdam on his 1770 tour, and here are his observations:

> I went to the new church, just at the time when the afternoon service was beginning; the building is lofty and noble; the organ which is partly gilt has a fine appearance, but no other use of it was made now, than to accompany the congregation in two long and tiresome Psalms, without either prelude or interlude, nor was the Psalm given out, as is usual in other places.[11]

He describes the key action on this organ as being particularly heavy. To depress a single key required a two-pound pressure, a requirement that would increase considerably when the manuals were coupled.

He also visited the Hague, where he found three Calvinistic churches and one Lutheran, all with organs.

Burney's observations seem to indicate that the use of the organ in church services, although officially approved by the Dutch Reformed

---

[10] Henry George Farmer, *op. cit.*, p. 277.
[11] Percy A. Scholes, *Dr. Burney's Musical Tours, etc.*, p. 225.

Church, had not made much headway since its official rehabilitation in 1636.

CHOIRS INTRODUCED TO SCOTLAND

The early part of the eighteenth century found Scotch church music at as low an ebb as it had been in the previous century. Neither organs nor choirs were permitted. In 1706 the General Assembly tried to interest its people in singing psalms in the homes. In 1713 an appeal was made to schoolteachers to assist their pupils in learning the "common tunes" of the Psalms. There is no evidence that either promotional scheme succeeded. For one thing, the church did not believe in engaging professional musicians to carry out its program. The general attitude toward the use of choral music in church is illustrated by the comments of a Scotch Presbyterian writing in 1754:

> A new-fangled profanation of the Sabbath was introduced by singing the psalms at Church with a herd-boy's whistle . . . which gives great offence to many serious Christians, which led to the innovation of singing music in parts by trained choristers, set apart by themselves in a loft or corner of the church, begun by a profane heretic above a thousand years ago.[12]

A fortuitous incident seems to have done much to change this attitude. An English soldier stationed at Aberdeen in 1753—a Mr. Channon, likely a Methodist—began after his discharge from the army to train choirs in the Monymusk area. Upon invitation, he brought one of his choirs to Aberdeen to demonstrate his work. A choir of twenty-two women and forty-eight men sang "in perfect harmony, and with the greatest exactness in time, very much to the satisfaction of a numerous audience."[13] His choir visited several congregations and was enthusiastically received, but the wrath of the church was soon upon him because he used music not found in *The Twelve Tunes for the Church of Scotland,* which was officially the only music to be used in church. In fact, all precentors had to promise on accepting the duties of their office that they would "sing only, in all time coming, the twelve church tunes commonly sung in Scotland."

Since the Anglican churches in Scotland already had choirs, Channon's activities added fuel to a smoldering fire that soon reached out to

---

[12] Henry George Farmer, *op. cit.,* p. 266.
[13] Millar Patrick, *Four Centuries of Scottish Psalmody* (London: Oxford, 1949), p. 153.

engulf all Scotch Presbyterians in a heated controversy. The pressure for change was coming from members of the congregations, and the church leaders could no longer cope with the situation. A number of choirs were organized, and one of their first functions was to introduce new melodies not contained in *The Twelve Tunes*. By 1778 the choir-movement seemed safely enough launched that Dr. James Beattie, a professor in Aberdeen, dared to opine that hymns, chanting, and anthems "might be performed in churches with the happiest effect." [14]

In some churches the choirs became so large that special lofts had to be built for them. John Wesley wrote in his *Journal* in 1761:

> About six we went to church. It was pretty well filled with such persons as we did not look for so near the Highlands. But if we were surprised at their appearance, we were more so at their singing. Thirty or forty sang an anthem after sermon, with such voices as well as judgment, that I doubt whether they could have been excelled at any Cathedral in England.[15]

While toward the end of the eighteenth century choirs were at least tolerated in some Scotch churches, organs were to be banned for another hundred years.

SWISS AND DUTCH CHORAL MUSIC

Some choral music was being used in Zürich, Switzerland, by the middle of the eighteenth century, mainly under the influence of a composer, Schmidlin, who resided there. Groups organized after the pattern of the *collegia musica* (prevalent a century earlier) sang in church after the service was over, although in a few communities some compositions by Sweelinck and other seventeenth-century composers were sung during worship.

Church choirs were not to be found in the Netherlands at this time. John Calvin's theological influence had kept music from playing a significant role in church life. The government even forbade Lutheran congregations to adopt the liturgical practices of German Lutherans, and their sole source of church music was the hymnal.

In the Reformed churches the Geneva Psalter was permitted, and by the middle of the eighteenth century the congregational singing could be accompanied on the organ.

---

[14] *Manual of Church Praise* (Edinburgh: The Church of Scotland Committee on Publications, 1932), p. 47.

[15] Millar Patrick, *op. cit.*, pp. 160-61.

ANGLICAN CHURCH MUSIC
THE CHOIR AND CHORAL MUSIC

Seventeenth-century English church music, with its suppression by the Puritans, its secular innovations under Charles II, its gallery musicians and its barrel organs was, charitably speaking, rather unstable. But the eighteenth century was to make no significant contribution at all. A number of factors probably contributed to this condition, one of which was the absence of any great composers.

George Frederick Handel, a German-born, Italian-trained musician, took up permanent residence here in 1712, and the English adopted him as their very own. He spent a lot of his time writing operas that have long since been forgotten, but he is remembered today by his choral works, notably his oratorio, *The Messiah,* first performed in 1742. The twenty-one other oratorios that Handel wrote have met the same fate as his forty-seven operas. His church music, like that of many German contemporaries, was *concert* music and was not written for use in church services. Although Handel and J. S. Bach were contemporaries and achieved success in the same general area, that of church music, yet they held differing points of view and had different purposes in mind. Handel, for his part, filled a vacuum in English music history. Some of the better English-born composers tried to imitate him, but their results were at best mediocre.

One of the better-known native composers of early eighteenth-century England was William Croft (1678-1727), whose main claim to fame is probably that familiar hymn tune St. Anne, to which we sing "O God, Our Help in Ages Past." But in addition to composing this number it was he who in 1724 published the *Musica Sacra,* a collection of thirty anthems and a real landmark in English cathedral music. A unique feature of this work was the engraving of the music on plates in *full score* rather than printing them in separate voice parts, which had been the custom previously. Croft felt that singers should have the advantage of seeing the complete score, and not just their individual voice parts.

Another of the century's few historic achievements in English choral music was the collecting, editing, and publishing of England's finest choral music from the early sixteenth century on. Previously the choral groups had been making handwritten copies of the selections they wanted to use, and over the years a great many errors had crept in. Thus a given composition might well be found in a wide variety of versions across the country.

The Herculean publishing task was first undertaken by John Alcock, one of the vicars choral at Lichfield Cathedral. Soon after making his intentions known, he learned that Maurice Greene, a teacher-composer-organist at St. Paul's in London, had set himself to the same task. Alcock thereupon turned over his materials to Greene, fully expecting that the latter would finish the job. But Dr. Greene died in 1755, before the work was finished, and his mantle fell upon William Boyce, one of his pupils, who was also an organist-composer of some stature.

The first volume of this monumental work, entitled *Cathedral Music,* was published in 1760. It was dedicated to King George II. The second volume followed in 1768 and the third in 1778. Croft's *Musica Sacra* now had some serious competition, for nothing like *Cathedral Music* had previously been available. A second edition was issued in 1788, and subsequent editions were published in the second half of the nineteenth century by J. Alfred Novello, son of the well-known music publisher Vincent Novello.

When Boyce died in 1779, English choral music began a fateful decline from which even today it has scarcely extricated itself. The musical situation was pathetic, and not just in the smaller churches. There were complaints about choirs of charity children, often numbering from fifty to a hundred, who strained their voices to the accompaniment of full organ but could never "raise the admiration of the performers" or create a sense of devotion among their hearers.

It was even worse in the smaller churches, who could not even boast a children's choir or an organ. In such instances, the "clerk" sang the announced hymn or psalm and would gain the following of a few feeble voices before he finished. A collection of psalms and hymns by a Rev. C. Dunster, prepared for the church he served from 1789 to 1816, contained the following singing rules:

1. The Clerk to give out the Psalm, distinctly, in his natural tone of voice.

2. The Organ, or Instrumental Band, to play the tune over once; the last note of which will be the key, or pitch note.

3. The Clerk then to give out the first line of the Psalm in the key note.

4. Then the congregation all standing up to sing the Psalm, within the compass of everyone's voice; and, where there is no Organ, without any instrumental accompaniment, except that of the Violoncello, and of some one other instrument, when it may be found necessary to regulate the voices of the boys.[16]

ORGAN IMPROVEMENTS

The organs in England in the eighteenth century were only slightly improved over the earlier instruments built by Schmidt and Harris. Not until 1790 were pedal organs being built in England—about four hundred years after they began appearing in Germany—and one of these was installed at St. James in Clerkenwell. It had an octave of pedal keys, but these did not control separate pipes. Handel, who died in 1759, had a particular fondness for the organ in St. Paul's Cathedral because in its day it was one of the few organs in England to have a set of pedals.

After the 1644 ban on organs had been lifted, it was a tedious, erratic, centuries-long process to get them reestablished. Most small village churches had no organs until the latter half of the nineteenth century—just a hundred years ago. The barrel organs and the gallery minstrels of the late seventeenth century continued to figure prominently in the smaller churches until well into the nineteenth century. Instrumental groups found wide use in the Anglican churches in the early eighteenth century, and in many communities they continued to find employment to the end of the century. Organists today who might feel dissatisfied with their lot or peeved at their difficult working conditions as compared with those of their successors might find some comfort in the experiences of John Alcock, the first compiler of *Cathedral Music*. While serving as parish organist in a church near Lichfield, he recorded:

'Tis incredible what a number of base artifices have been practised by some people belonging to this cathedral, in order to prejudice me in my profession, and to distress my family for no cause whatever . . . albeit the salary *then* was *only* four pounds *per* annum, besides the Vicar's place, and there was much more *duty* when I was organist *than now,* being obliged always to play a voluntary after Morning and Evening Prayers, even in the severest cold weather, when, very often, there was only one Vicar, who read the service, and an old woman at church beside the choristers; which not only brought, but fixed, the rheumatism so strongly upon me that I am seldom free from pain, and

---

[16] Canon K. H. MacDermott, *op. cit.,* p. 60.

sometimes confined to my bed for eight or ten days together. . . . All the time I was organist, which was upwards of ten years, there was not a book in the organloft fit for use, but what I bought or wrote myself (for which I was never paid one halfpenny), and yet there have been as many books purchased within the last few years, as have cost, at least, thirty guineas.[17]

In spite of the backwardness of English church music at this time, there were a few cases where superb music had a chance to develop. The following account of John Beckwith (1750-1809), organist at Norwich Cathedral and renowned for his improvisations, reminds one of the impeccable Reinkin of Hamburg, whom J. S. Bach frequently heard. Being handed the subject of a fugue during the sermon he would improvise the composition as a postlude at the close of the service. After having given out the subject

and replied to it in the regular way, he would treat it, if possible, by inversion, reversion, augmentation, and diminution, carrying it through a course of modulation till he came to the *Knot,* when he would bring the replies in closer and closer, until his hearers were in raptures with delight.[18]

METHODIST CHURCH MUSIC

There remains one area of English church music yet to consider: that of the Methodists. The first organ to be installed in a Methodist chapel in England was in the New King Street Chapel in Bath. This was in 1779, soon after the chapel was built. John Wesley (1703-1791), the founder of Methodism, was sincerely interested in music and had some acquaintance with it. Upon having an opportunity to hear the organ at a communion service in a Manchester church, very appropriately played by a Mr. Maclardie, he informed the organist after the service that if he could be assured that all organists would perform as tastefully and well as he had, he would place an organ in every one of his chapels.

Instrumental music in general was of little importance to the Methodists, however. The bass viol was perhaps the first used, followed by the clarinet and several other instruments. Organs were officially forbidden by the Wesley group in 1796, although twelve years later some organs were being installed. Introducing an organ was the cause of strife in more than one congregation.

---

[17] John S. Bumpus, *op. cit.,* pp. 347–48.
[18] *Ibid.,* p. 354.

Choral music fared little better. The use of anthems was forbidden in 1786 because they were considered inappropriate for corporate worship. When John Wesley visited a Warrington church in 1781 and found men with good voices singing a Psalm which no one knew, in a musical setting based on a tune fit for an opera, he regarded this as a "burlesque upon public worship." It so repelled him, in fact, that he banned such singing from the Methodist service.

Some music did exist sporadically among the Methodists, although officially this group did not favor the use of organs, choirs, or a group of instruments. The only "legal" instrument was the bass viol.

V

The Century of
Nascent Reform

IN GERMANY AND NEIGHBORING AREAS

In the half century following the death of J. S. Bach in 1750, the decline of European church music, already begun, now continued unabated. Many cantors were dismissed from their posts, choirs were disbanded, some churches curtailed the use of organs. Secular musicians held many of the church positions, and instrumental music was gaining in prominence. As the nineteenth century dawned, it seemed as though anything that might happen in church music would be an improvement.

In Switzerland and the Netherlands the nineteenth century would see little activity in the areas of our concern in this book. Both organs and choirs remained somewhat in disrepute. Lutheran congregations in the Netherlands did use special choirs for the more festive occasions, and the Dutch Reformed churches included some Dutch hymns in their psalm books that could be sung by the congregation, which was a harbinger of later reform.

In Germany, early 18th-century pietism had raised havoc with the virile Reformation melodies, often turning them into flowery, waltz-like tunes. The extreme reaction against this, under nineteenth-century rationalism, rendered the same melodies completely devoid of any vitality. The following examples will illustrate these points. From Freylinghausen's famous pietistic hymnal of 1741:

From E. Hentschel's *Evangelisches Choralbuch* published in 1860:

It will be noted that the latter contains an example of *Zwischenspiel*.

These transformations—neither of which does justice to the original chorale melody—are well summed up in a simple statement by Paul Henry Lang:

> The "spiritual songs" [of pietism] which displaced the magnificent treasure of Protestant church melodies led to the arbitrarily set, gloomy, and dragging congregational singing that was a caricature of the sturdy and lively chorales of the heroic age of the Reformation.[1]

---

[1] Paul Henry Lang, *op. cit.*, p. 701.

In addition to the onslaughts of pietism and rationalism, church music was also subjected to secular influences, mainly from Italian opera. *Performances* of music took place in churches by choirs accompanied by orchestras in the grand style of the theatre, but music as an act of worship seemed to be the concern of no one. And congregational singing had nearly ceased to exist.

The beginning of a church music renaissance is noticeable in the publication of the *Berliner Gesangbuch* in 1829, which embodied some reforms from rationalism. But this was only a beginning, and not a very pronounced one at that. The next fifty years witnessed several more steps in a different direction, but even toward the close of the nineteenth century much remained to be accomplished.

Church choirs, if they existed at all, were of a decidedly inferior grade. The music they sang was generally very poor in quality, secular in style, and of no liturgical significance. As late as 1885 there were very few church choirs. The five churches in the city of Augsburg had only one choir among them, and this sang on a rotation plan. The age had its share of well-known composers—Brahms, Strauss, Reger, Bruckner—but these did little for church music.

The organists fared better than the choirs during this period, but they too were preoccupied with non-church music. In 1823 a ministerial order was issued in Baden, forbidding the organist to play *Zwischenspiel* or to employ any sort of ornamentations or variations while accompanying congregational singing (what little of it there was!). Similarly in 1820 the Magdeburg Church and School Commission gave directions that nothing was to be played on the organ that militated against the dignity of the service. Secular music—ballad tunes, marches, dances—were specifically forbidden.

By 1850 the pattern was well established: the organist was to play an opening prelude, a selection during the offering, and a postlude. The use of *Zwischenspiel* at the end of each verse line was still an "in" practice. The music of J. S. Bach was beginning to reappear outside the pale of Lutheranism at this time.

An Englishman, John S. Curwen, made this notation in 1863, following a church service he attended in Göttingen:

> The congregation sings draggingly and indolently; if they sing at all they sing with all their might, and as the throats are differently organized, and there is no sufficient guidance, every individual voice gets its own way, and the whole follows the law of inertia as necessar-

ily as a heap of rolling sand. The organist is forced to take the reins into his hands, and he has no other means of keeping the singing together and directing it than a heavy and broad organ accompaniment, which, if it has not the desired effect, at all events, prevents the congregation from singing still louder.[2]

It was to rectify such calamitous conditions that a tremendous amount of church music research was carried out from midcentury onward. The *Eisenach Choralbuch*, issued at this time, was an attempt to give all provincial chorale books a common nucleus of selections and to counteract the diversity that had reigned until now. Another important publication for the organists was Friedrich Layriz's *Kern des deutschen Kirchengesangs*. Layriz, revolting against rationalism, used more rhythmic variety in the melodies and suggested that the *Zwischenspiel* be restricted to the ends of stanzas rather than appearing after each verse line.

Organ music, like choral music, was simply not being written at this time. A few compositions by Mendelssohn and Rheinberger could be considered usable in worship, but these were the exception to the rule.

IN SCANDINAVIA

Nineteenth-century church music in Scandinavia fared much the same as in Germany, with two basic differences: (1) most of the leaders in musical affairs were either Germans or else Scandinavian nationals who had studied in Germany; (2) native musical traditions and musical composition were barely under way by the early nineteenth century. The first Norwegian composers of any stature had appeared on the scene very late in the eighteenth century, among these being Lars M. Ibsen (b. 1780).

In 1838 Norwegian organists did receive their first chorale book to be prepared by a *bona fide* Norwegian, O. A. Lindeman, who was organist in the Vor Frue Church in Trondheim and the greatest Norwegian organist of his time. (Of course, there were very few organists in Norway then.) Lindeman's chorale book replaced a similar work published 1801 by an immigrant German, H. C. O. Zinck, whose chorale settings were in the traditional even-note rhythmic pattern so characteristic of German composition at the time. According to Sandvik, the Norwegian church-music historian,

---

[2] John S. Curwen, *Studies in Worship Music, Second Series* (London: J. Curwen, 1885), pp. 146-47.

96

Zinck's chorale book is used by the organist but he ornaments the melody with an endless number of trills, figurations, and interludes which often remind us of dances with which he regales us as the parish musician. . . . He plays for his own enjoyment, and fermatas become stopping places which stretch out by the minute.[3]

Many stories are told about the "virtuosi" organists of this period, of which the following will serve as typical:

An organist sees the words *fear* and *dread* coming in the hymn which is being sung. Immediately he pulls out the tremolo stop, lays to with both arms over all the keys, and sets both feet on the pedals. With this frightful howling and noise, not only does the congregation become completely terrified, but the poor fellow who treads the bellows has become almost crazy, for he fears that all the bellows will burst.[4]

O. A. Lindeman's chorale book, which he compiled after completing his studies at Copenhagen, was not much of an improvement over that of Zinck's. Congregational singing was at a critically low ebb, and Lindeman's chorale book had to shoulder much of the blame because it had become the only publication of its kind that was authorized for use in church. Others preferred to blame the poor singing on the use of the organ and the choir in the service.

The authorized chorale book has without doubt many shortcomings; its rhythm has neither life nor warmth. But it is difficult to give it all the blame for the inarticulateness of the church song. One of the reasons for the poor condition of the music must be found in introducing the organ into church and the deafening choir, with which the congregation becomes accustomed to consider the church song as being irrelevant.[5]

O. A. Lindeman's son Ludwig, organist at *Vor Frelsers* Kirke in Christiania (now Oslo), was the second to prepare a Norwegian chorale book, and in this he sought to rectify his father's shortcomings by giving the melodies greater rhythmic variety and by using more varied harmonies. Immediately after its publication in 1871 it was put into use, and it remained the official chorale book for the Norwegian Lutheran Church until the twentieth century.

The Norwegian choirs of this period were made up mainly of students who received "song money" for singing upon request at funerals, weddings, and other special occasions.

---

[3] O. M. Sandvik, *Norsk Koralhistoria* (Oslo: H. Aschehoug, 1930), p. 36.
[4] Fredrick Storm, *Traek af den religiöse Musiks og Orglets Historia* (Trondheim: T. A. Höeg, 1845), p. 56.
[5] O. M. Sandvik, *op. cit.,* p. 38.

Before the close of the nineteenth century the organ situation began to improve, although not to the satisfaction of Fredrick Storm, who complained in 1845:

> Nowadays one hears so many appeals to assist and promote other fine arts but about music nothing is said. Surely, this has a greater number of adherents. But of religious music, about church music and organ playing—and to what height this art can be promoted, and the influence it can exert in many directions—about such matters one in our country has only a poor conception. . . . Many pastors, because of a lack of knowledge in this area, are obliged to let this go its own erratic way, and carelessness, like all evil, is contagious.[6]

The Swedish counterpart of O. A. Lindeman was J. C. F. Haeffner, who besides being director of the Stockholm opera and court musician was organist at the German church in Stockholm. Haeffner's 1808 chorale book and the expanded sequel to this in 1820-21 set the stage for almost a century of strife over singing in the churches. Haeffner, a German, used many melodies from two recently published German chorale books—all promoting the even time-value notes so characteristic of O. A. Lindeman, whereas native Scandinavian melodies possessed considerable rhythmic variety. The people openly rebelled against such an innovation, and parents often compelled their children to swear by the Bible not to sing such melodies. This attitude was bound to have repercussions, not only on church music but on the nation's musical culture as a whole. By the end of the century reforms got under way, but the Haeffner influence has continued to hang like a dark shadow over developments, even in our own day.

Danish church music at the dawn of the nineteenth century was no exception to the Scandinavian rule. Niels Schiørring's chorale book, issued 1783, became the model for those who published such material as late as the early twentieth century. Fermatas at the ends of phrases were a signal for the organist to add his own little interludes, which were welcome relaxation from the stiff, plodding all-half-note movements of the chorale melodies. For prelude and postlude he played operatic overtures, marches, and waltzes, since the composers of his day were incapable of writing music appropriate for church use. Toward the end of the century a more wholesome situation seems to have existed in the smaller rural churches, where it was common for the schoolmaster to serve as organist and for a group of schoolchildren to

---

[6] Frederick Storm, *op. cit.*, pp. 75-76.

lead the congregational singing. The larger city churches often used a precentor, assisted by a choir of schoolchildren, whose function was to lead the congregational singing rather than to sing special selections of part music. Copenhagen toward the end of the century had a paid mixed choir of 10-16 adults who sang several parts of the liturgy.

Iceland made her first strides in church music during this century. The Reykjavik Cathedral got its first pipe organ in 1840. Pjetur Guojohnsen, the cathedral organist at that time, prepared Iceland's first modern-notation chorale book in 1861. This book contained only the melodies, but Guojohnsen's successor Johan Helgason prepared a four-voice chorale book that appeared in 1887. Many smaller churches used harmoniums instead of pipe organs.

There was little choral activity in Iceland yet, due to the country's lag in musical development and the limited reportoire of its choral music.

IN SCOTLAND

THE ORGAN CONTROVERSY

The most exciting activities in nineteenth-century church music were to be found in Scotland, where the tenacious opposition of Scotch churchmen was being undermined by the musical activities of the Anglican churches in their midst, which appealed in particular to the Scottish youth. But church officialdom still denied that organs and choirs filled any need in worship.

The pressures continued to mount, however, as Anglican organists assumed the leadership of musical activities in their respective communities. Organ concerts were given in both Glasgow and Edinburgh, and Anglican trained choirs exerted a tremendous influence on Presbyterian ideas. Finally in 1845 the Congregational Church in Edinburgh followed the example of the Anglicans and installed an organ.

Meanwhile, a number of organ builders were becoming established in Scotland, making it unnecessary to import organs from England. Many of the instruments they built in the early part of the century were for home rather than church use. The pedalboard, already introduced to England by 1790, was unknown in Scotland for another half-century. In 1841 no organ in Edinburgh had pedals.

When the first Presbyterian organ was installed in 1804 at St. Andrew's in Glasgow, some held that this was not only subversive to church principles but illegal as well:

The first attempt to introduce an organ into divine worship in the Church of Scotland appears to have been made in St. Andrew's church, Glasgow, at the beginning of the nineteenth century. The instrument in question had been made by the famous James Watt, and had come into the possession of the Kirk-Session of St. Andrew's. It was used at the weekly rehearsal of congregational praise, and the minister, Dr. Ritchie, conceived the idea of employing it at divine service on Sundays, a proposal which seems to have received the hearty support of the congregation. Accordingly in 1806 a petition was presented to the Town Council of Glasgow, as Patrons and Heritors of the church, craving permission to remove certain seats in the church in order to make room for the organ. The petition was refused; but the proposal to introduce the instrument into divine service was not allowed to drop, and in the following year the first step was taken by employing it one Sunday to accompany the concluding Psalm. The innovation caused a great commotion in the city. The Town Council called upon the Presbytery to intervene, and after much discussion that court declared the use of an organ contrary to the law of the land, and to the law and constitution of the Established Church, and prohibited it in all churches and chapels within their bounds.

As Dr. Ritchie had undertaken not to continue the use of the instrument while the subject was under discussion, the actual employment of the organ on this occasion was limited to the accompaniment of a single Psalm at one diet of worship. It was not till after the middle of the century that the question of introducing instrumental music was revived, and to Dr. Robert Lee of Old Greyfriars, Edinburgh, belongs the honor of having carried through this and other reforms in the conduct of divine service. . . . He . . . had a harmonium to support the Psalmody. These innovations caused considerable stir, and the matter came before the General Assembly of 1864. In spite of the contention of those opposed to the movement that such innovations were contrary to the law of the Church, it was decided that they were to be forbidden only when they caused dispeace in the congregation. The practice of having instrumental music spread, and in course of time it became the general custom.[7]

One would expect such a major change to meet some strong opposition, in view of a clause contained in the ordination service of Presbyterian ministers which made them promise to "defend the purity of worship as presently practiced." The Presbyterian philosophy was that nothing should be admitted to the service unless it had scriptural authority, whereas Lutherans felt that almost anything was permissible in worship if it was not expressly forbidden by Scripture, which is why

---

[7] G. W. Stewart, *op. cit.,* pp. 156-57.

Lutherans had no compunctions about using organs and choirs in their worship services.

The Presbyterians appealed to numerous passages of Scripture, including Matthew 28:20: "Teaching them to observe all things whatsoever I have commanded you." Obviously the New Testament did not *command* the use of organs in worship!

The Glasgow Presbytery ruled against the use of organs in its churches and chapels, but the city's legal advisor insisted that there was no legislative prohibition against the use of organs, although he allowed the argument that introducing an organ into the church was a material alteration and that as an innovation in the mode of worship could be construed as "disturbing the peace" and bringing discord into the life of the church. This final opinion, however, was that those who criticized the organ—as they had already opposed the pitch pipe— should not be taken too seriously.

Much of the controversy over the organ was carried on in the printed form of pamphlets and books. In *The Organ Question* by a Dr. Ritchie and a Dr. Porteous, published 1856, Dr. Ritchie expressed himself for the use of the organ and Dr. Porteous was against it. A considerable amount of printer's ink was consumed before the "battle of the bellows" came to an end.

A second battlefront developed at about the same time in Edinburgh, where an organ was installed in 1828. The justification given was that the Church of Scotland had already installed organs in their Calcutta and Jamaica churches!

The synod exerted pressure for the removal of the Edinburgh organ, the net result being that both pastor and congregation severed their affiliation with the synod, which led to a new series of pamphlets for and against the use of the organ. Among these were *An Apology for the Organ as an Assistance of Congregational Psalmody*, published in 1829, and *Instrumental Music in Public Worship*, published the same year. *The Sacrifice of Praise*, published 1858 in Glasgow, advocated the use of the organ as being in accordance with Scripture. *A Vindication of the Organ* appeared 1866 in Edinburgh and in the same year *The Use of Organs and Other Instruments of Music in Christian Worship Indefensible* was published in Glasgow. The last-named volume was written specifically for Presbyterians, the author's basic premise being that just because the New Testament does not expressly forbid the use of organs this does not mean we should feel free to use them! Pointing out that the history of musical instruments is closely connected with the progress and triumph of idolatry, superstition, and cruelty, the author observes that

> if we introduce instrumental music in our New Testament worship, we cannot plead either the precept or example of Christ or His apostles. . . . If art is used at all in connection with religion—for example, in the use of choirs, or the erection of superior ecclesiastical buildings—it may as well be used in the employment of instrumental music in the worship of God. If this argument were admitted, it is difficult to see what limit could be set to its application.[8]

There were those, however, who felt that one should make the place of worship as attractive and presentable as possible, so long as the act of beautification was not directly countermanded by God. Resistance to the organ gradually became inarticulate, and when the aforementioned Dr. Robert Lee of Edinburgh introduced the use of a harmonium to Old Grayfriars in 1863, it apparently caused very few hard feelings, for it was only a few years more until an organ was installed. It became increasingly difficult to keep the individual congregations in line. In Glasgow, for example, a United Presbyterian church installed an organ in 1855, but it could not be used until the synod gave its consent, which was seventeen years later!

A sincere effort was made in the second half of the nineteenth century to bring order out of chaos. In 1866 the Established Church in Scotland authorized organs, followed by the United Presbyterian Church in Scotland (1872). The Free Church finally (1883) allowed organs because they could find no Scripture or church law that forbade their use.

It is understandable, in view of all this, that church music among Scotch Presbyterians should be rather mediocre throughout most of the nineteenth century. Psalm-singing, it is true, was a regular feature of Scotch worship, but the editors of the Scotch psalters had for the most part been musically incompetent since the early 17th century. The result was a lot of inferior melodies and wrongly copied notes. By mid-nineteenth century there were improvements: A few churches were using small groups of special singers to lead the congregation in their singing of the psalms, but this practice was considered objection-

---

[8] James Begg, *The Use of Organs and Other Instruments of Music in Christian Worship Indefensible* (Glasgow & London: W. R. M'Phun, 1866), pp. 18, 48.

able by the majority. Since church music was controlled by the clergy, a Glasgow precentor was led to observe in 1858 that few church officials and even fewer ministers knew anything about music. This situation was remedied to some extent by providing the precentors with instruction books in the rudiments of music, to be used for their own self-training and for the teaching of psalm tunes to schoolchildren and congregations.

CHOIRS IN SCOTLAND

Considering that choral work got off to such a poor start among the Scotch Presbyterians, it is interesting to note the continued development of this infant art during the nineteenth century. In the early part of the century, a few anthems were being included in some church publications, such as Dr. Andrew Thomson's *Sacred Harmony,* published 1820. In 1875 the Church of Scotland published a collection specifically for use by the choir, but by this time there was a sizable amount of choir literature available elsewhere. The precentor and choirmaster at St. Giles Cathedral, for example, had prepared *Words of Anthems Used in St. Giles,* and only forty-four of its nearly four hundred anthems were to be found in the church-authorized collection. But by most standards the 1875 anthology was a good collection of music, containing compositions by Byrd, Gibbons, Purcell, J. S. Bach, Mozart, Handel, Mendelssohn, and some other outstanding composers. Another church-authorized collection, *The Scottish Anthem Book,* was published in 1891.

The United Presbyterians moved somewhat more cautiously than the Church of Scotland. In 1876 they appended twenty-four "Scripture Sentences" to *The Presbyterian Hymnal,* and ten years later they issued *Scripture Sentences and Chants,* containing 107 anthems.

The Free Church also appended a collection of "Sentences" to its 1882 hymnal, and in 1905 the United Free Church (a merger of Free Church and United Presbyterians) authorized a collection of 166 anthems.

These publications demonstrate that there was considerable activity in church music before the nineteenth century came to a close. Many an older composition found in some cathedral library was prepared for republication, and hitherto unpublished music was also made available.

IN ENGLAND

THE ORGAN

Handel's death in 1759 left English music in the same sort of vacuum it had known before his arrival, and, what is more, his "church music" was designed for concert performance rather than for use in worship. There were no native English composers to set the pace, and no significant reform measures were instituted until very late in the nineteenth century. The Georgian era (1714-1830) had been unfavorably disposed toward ecclesiastical art in general and music in particular. Organists and composers in the pay of cathedrals, college chapels, and chapels royal, while doing what they could to keep church music alive, probably despaired under the circumstances of making it any better.

Relatively few organs were yet to be found in small-town Anglican churches of the mid-nineteenth century. Other church groups—Methodists, Independents, and Baptists—had only a few organs per denomination, and the Presbyterians were strongly opposed to using them at all. About 1815 a group from the Methodist Brunswick Chapel in Leeds decided to install an organ, but found that the clergy and other churchmen of the community were opposed to the move. They sought permission from the district officials, but again it was denied them, after which they took their case to the conference level and received a favorable decision.

Organs with pedalboards became more common in England during the first half of the century. In 1834 an organ built at York had two octaves of pedals. Several organs built in this period had pedals that operated special sets of pipes. But as late as 1884 Dr. Longhurst, organist at the Canterbury Cathedral, mentioned that his instrument had only one octave of pedals. Since so many English-built organs had at best only a short pedalboard, one can understand why Bach's organ music was virtually unknown. Many organists would have nothing to do with pedals. When Sir George Smart, organist at the Chapel Royal, was asked to try an organ equipped with pedals built for the 1851 London Exhibition, he replied: "My dear Sir, I never in my life played on a gridiron."

In addition to the barrel organ, which had gained so much notoriety in the previous century, two other types of organ now became popular, particularly in the small churches: (1) the so-called American organ, and (2) the harmonium. What the English call the American organ was actually a reed organ, probably modeled after those developed in 1860 by Mason and Hamlin of Boston. The harmonium, first developed in France about 1810, did not find general use in England until 1840, but by 1850 it began replacing the gallery minstrels. The term "pair of organs" is frequently met with in the English literature of this period, and refers to organs that had an extended downward compass. Churches possessing barrel organs did not necessarily give these up in favor of one of the newer instruments. Some churches actually retained them to the end of the century.

By mid-century many of the smaller churches had no organs of any kind. In 1853 a rural deanery in Sussex comprising seventeen churches had only three organs, and these seem to have been quite recently acquired. By 1878 the possession of an organ was still an optional matter, and was required only for cathedrals and collegiate churches.

One bright spot in the history of this century was the improvement the English made in organ building—particularly their addition of pedalboards. This did not mean that the organist gained any status in the community. It was a tradition of long standing for the minister to be in complete control of his parish and to bear full responsibility even for church music. Church law gave no official recognition either to the choir director or to the organist.

One item in the reform of organ music should be noted: By 1880 the playing of interludes (*Zwischenspiel*) between verse lines had disappeared from general practice.

The non-Anglican churches of England moved gradually in the direction of introducing organs before the century was over. The English Presbyterians had installed a couple by 1866, the same year that they were authorized for use in Scotland. By 1872 the United Presbyterians in Scotland permitted organs, but the same group in England continued the debate for a while. Indicative of how some people felt is the comment that organs "are often played so loudly that the choir and congregation chirp like birds in a thunderstorm." [9] By the end of the century nearly all Methodist churches had organs.

Dr. Robert S. Candlish, in his preface to *The Organ Question* (published Edinburgh, 1856) gives what is obviously a biased view because of his personal opposition to the organ:

---

[9] John S. Curwen, *op. cit.*, p. 87.

In the Church of England all sorts of hymns are allowed, and the service conducted in all sorts of styles, from the richest ritualism to the baldest and tamest routine. On the Congregational system, every pastor with his people may take his own way—one using instrumental music, and another condemning the use of it. . . . Those Presbyterians who disapprove, on conscientious and spiritual grounds, of a particular mode of worship—as, for instance, of the organ—cannot divest themselves of responsibility merely by excluding it from their own congregation. . . . All who are conscientiously opposed to it—who regard it as inexpedient and unlawful, unauthorised and unscriptural, must feel themselves bound as Presbyterians *to do their utmost against a proposal to have it ever tolerated.*[10]

In 1833 England saw the beginnings of the Oxford Movement, which revived earlier doctrines and practices of the Church of England. Surpliced choirs of men and boys were now placed *in the chancel* of the church and were accompanied by an organ or harmonium placed near by. Since many churches had no room in their chancels for a choir or an organ, the church architects began designing new buildings with this in mind.

In 1892 H. S. Shuttleworth concluded that this innovation was less than desirable:

Like the choir, the organ has suffered sadly by being brought down from the gallery at the west end, where it was a great architectural feature of the church until the Puritans smashed the noble old organ cases of carven woodwork. Our modern architects, with perverse disregard of acoustics, almost always place the organ on one side of the chancel, in a sort of box or cupboard, which they term an 'organ chamber.' They might as well put it in the steeple.[11]

THE CHOIR

Following the Handelian period in England, church choral music had little popular appeal to the people. There was more interest in the spectacular type of concert music performed by large groups, making it financially risky to publish shorter selections suitable for worship purposes. To make matters worse, there were music "editors" who resorted to publishing mutilated versions of certain standard choruses, including several from Handel's *The Messiah*. "Rejoice Greatly," for example, is 108 measures in length but was published in a 52-measure

---

[10] James Begg, *op. cit.,* pp. 140, 141.
[11] H. S. Shuttleworth, *The Place of Music in Public Worship* London: Elliot Stock, 1892), pp. 56, 57.

version. "For unto Us a Child Is Born," 99 measures in length, **was** reduced to 70 measures. In 1826 the English author John Antes **La** Trobe brought four charges against the choir and the organist:

1. *Want of reverence.* This, he felt, applied to both the choir **and** the organist. With the exception of some small country churches, **the** practice was to keep the choir rather secluded by drawing a curtain **to** shield them from the audience. This encouraged choir members **to** carry on conversations in an undertone, to rustle the pages of **their** songbooks, and to pay very little attention to the service. The **author** also felt that admitting women to the choir had been the source **of** much impropriety. "What can be more unpleasing," he asks, "than to see a female with unabashed front, standing up in the presence of the full congregation, and with outstretched neck, screaming above the voices of the multitude, and the swell of the organ, like a seagull in a tempest!"

The organist would often while away the time by engaging in "pantomimic exercises upon his instrument, eagerly thrumming the voiceless keys, and stamping upon the unanswering pedals." This would seem a harmless enough diversion, but it underestimated the man working the bellows, who might at any minute give in to the mischievous impulse to start pumping!

2. *Fondness for display.* This criticism was aimed particularly at the organist, who often attracted the attention of worshipers by "some theatrical exhibition, and his ear filled with the unecclesiastical materiel of some wanton saraband."

3. *Obstinate rejection of advice.* Failure to understand the design and nature of the service was a common failing of the organist. Added to this, his conceit and ignorance often hindered him from accepting the minister's advice.

4. *Bad taste.* Much poor music was being sung, and good music was being poorly sung. Choir members were often recruits from the theatre and opera who had no interest in worship music for its own sake. The organist would "crowd a chorale, the burden of which is best understood by the absence of every kind of decoration, with such a multitude of turns, flourishes, interludes, shakes, trills, appoggiaturas, and other expletive notes, that the unfortunate tune is totally overwhelmed under a mass of ill-judged musical commentary." [12]

---

[12] John Antes La Trobe, *The Music of the Church* (London: L. B. Seeley, 1831), pp. 114-37.

Eric Routley, an eminent Scottish theologian of our own day and author of several books on church music, has this to say about the poor quality of nineteenth-century church music:

> But this music, the secular music of the salon, was not the final degradation. It remained for the Church to debase music to the limit. For music designed to create mere natural emotions such as sorrow or pity, or peace of mind has at any rate what a celebrated broadcaster calls "animal content." But the hack-music of the church, of which our hymnals are still full, and which our churches are only now beginning to abandon, music designed to produce not natural emotion but (save the mark) religious emotion—this was music at its lowest ebb.
>
> Victorian church music . . . can be described as music which occasionally rises to greatness, often achieves a serviceable character, but which is prone to diverge from even the serviceable ideal in the directions either of supreme tedium or of shameless vulgarity.[13]

This was the century of such well-known English composers as Thomas Attwood Walmisley (1814-56), Samuel S. Wesley (1810-76), Henry Smart (1813-79), John Goss (1800-80), Frederick A. G. Ouseley (1825-89) and John Stainer (1840-1901). Of these, Routley rates Walmisley and Wesley as being the best, with Smart being "the least capable of either greatness or indiscretion."

About the middle of the nineteenth century, the quartet was introduced by Henry W. Greatorex, organist at Hartford. A number of churches soon followed his example. The innovation could hardly be classified as a "step forward." The quartet members, as a rule, were four individualistic soloists who "turned out weak and sentimental ditties to tickle the ears of the musically ignorant, and to afford each of the soloists an opportunity for personal display." [14]

As the nineteenth century entered its second half, English church music remained about as meaningless and trite as ever. The composers, capable of doing much better, ignored the traditions established by earlier English composers and tried to imitate men like Gounod and Spohr, who visited from abroad. Samuel S. Wesley managed to counteract this tendency somewhat by modifying the structure of the anthem. He added a free organ accompaniment that moved independently of the voice parts. His *A Few Words on Cathedral Music*

---

[13] Erik Routley, *op. cit.*, p. 180.
[14] George Gardner and Sydney H. Nicholson, *A Manual of English Church Music* (London: SPCK, 1936), pp. 4, 5.

(published 1849) also stirred interest in some type of reform. His enthusiasm for reestablishing the English choral Eucharist led to a rediscovery of the works of earlier English composers. Other reform measures were instigated by Sir John Stainer, in 1872 appointed organist at St. Paul's. These were significant "straws in the wind" but a definite and sustained movement toward reform did not crystalize until about 1880. The willingness to experiment is evident in at least one case, when the choir was dispersed through the congregation and sang from where they sat. It suggested that the entire congregation should feel themselves part of the choir and should participate with the choir in the music of the service.

Continued improvement in English church music was evident as the century came to a close. The choristers at St. Matthias in Stoke Newington must have had a sense of responsibility and devotion to their work, for no one was accepted into choir membership there unless he promised to meet with the group twice on Sundays and three evenings during the week. This organization sang Evensong daily, besides singing at the Sunday services, and was under the direction of William Monk (1823-1889), who also composed a number of hymns, including the familiar "Abide with Me."

By the end of the century there were an increasing number of male choruses, even in the small towns and villages, and these had without question a higher set of musical standards than the eighteenth-century gallery minstrels.

VI

Beginnings of Church
Music in America

THE EIGHTEENTH CENTURY
THE FIRST ORGANS IN AMERICA

Much of the early history of organs in America is a matter of conjecture, since there are few records to be relied on. It is evident, however, that before 1737 any organs in use here would have been imported, mainly or exclusively from England.

Reputedly the first time an organ was used in a worship service was in 1703, at the ordination of Justus Falckner, a Lutheran, in what is now Philadelphia. But Percy Scholes [1] claims that the Episcopal church in Port Royal, Virginia, had an organ in 1700, although it may not have been used for services. Most historians also maintain that the Gloria Dei Swedish Lutheran Church, site of Falckner's ordination, did not have an organ in 1703, whereas Scholes suggests they could have had one installed as early as 1694. At any rate, the organ used at Falckner's ordination service is generally thought to have been a portable instrument, brought to the church for this specific occasion, and other circumstances lend credence to this position. Johannis Kelpius, who arrived in Philadelphia in 1649, is known to have ordered some clavichords from Europe in 1708, and an organ is mentioned in his writings. Some friends of his were invited to play and sing at the ordination service, and they brought along viols, oboes, trumpets, and

---

[1] Percy A. Scholes, *Oxford Companion to Music*, p. 664.

kettledrums, so it is reasonable to suppose they could have brought a portable organ as well.

If the church had no organ of its own at this time, Falckner may well have supplied the instrument himself. In 1701 he wrote to a church official in Schleswig (then in Denmark) requesting assistance, especially for an organ to be placed in the Swedish church. He argued that

a well-sounding organ would perhaps prove of great profit, to say nothing of the fact that the Indians would come running from far and near to listen to such unknown melody.[2]

The first recorded church action to purchase an organ was in 1704, by the vestry at Trinity Church in New York. The initial recommendation was not carried out, however, until 1737, when the instrument was finally installed. The Thomas Brattle organ was the first to be permanently installed in New England. Brattle, a Bostonian, had imported the organ in 1711 for use in his home, but bequeathed it to the Brattle Street Congregational Church. Upon his death in 1713, the church (not considered exactly conservative) refused to accept the instrument, whereupon it was given to the Episcopal Queens Chapel (later called Kings Chapel) according to instructions laid down in Brattle's will. The Brattle Street church did not install an organ until 75 years later, but even then a wealthy member of the congregation offered to pay the cost of the instrument to have it removed.

The second congregation to install an organ was probably the Dutch Reformed Church of New York. The organ was a gift from Governor Burnet in 1724. Christ Church in Philadelphia installed an organ in 1728; Trinity Church, Newport, in 1733. Both Trinity Church and Christ Church in Boston imported organs in 1736. An English organ, installed 1764 in Christ Church of Cambridge, Massachusetts, later had most of its lead pipes melted down to make bullets for the battle of Bunker Hill.

Episcopalians were usually the first to install organs in their churches. For the American colonists the purchase of an organ was a major financial undertaking, and often it was also necessary to import an organist to play it, as was the case when the Brattle organ was installed. By the end of the eighteenth century there were only about

---

[2] *Church Music and Musical Life in Pennsylvania in the Eighteenth Century* (Philadelphia: Committee on Historical Research of the Pennsylvania Society of the Colonial Dames of America, 1926), p. 173.

twenty organs (mostly in Episcopal churches) to be found in all New England—five built here and the rest imported from England. One of the largest organ installations of the century was in 1768 at St. Michael's Church, Charleston, South Carolina. It was a three-manual instrument with about 1,000 pipes, built by John Snetzler, a German who had settled in London shortly after 1740.

Outside Episcopalian circles, there were very few church organ installations during the eighteenth century. When instruments were used at all, they were usually string or wind instruments or combinations thereof. The Quakers and Presbyterians in Pennsylvania were opposed to any use of music in the church, even though they fostered its use in their homes and participated in chamber music groups. The first "dissenting" church in America to install an organ was the Congregational Church of Providence, in 1770. But the descendants of the Puritans eventually abandoned psalm-singing and began to install organs.

In 1763 William Dunlap, a Presbyterian minister, published a pamphlet in Philadelphia promoting the use of the organ by Presbyterians and Baptists. It bore the following inscription:

> The lawfulness, excellency and advantage of instrumental musick in the public worship of God, urg'd and enforc'd, from Scripture, and the examples of the far greater part of Christians in all ages. Address'd to all (particularly the Presbyterians and Baptists) who have hitherto been taught to look upon the use of instrumental musick in the worship of God as unlawful.[3]

As was already mentioned, trained organists were scarce at this time, and so were chorale books. It was especially difficult to get the books from Europe, so that organists often had to prepare their own handwritten copies, many of which were still being used in the early twentieth century.

ORGAN-BUILDERS

A number of organ-builders were active well before the middle of the century. Gustavus Hesselius arrived from Sweden in 1711 and built spinets in Philadelphia. He may have assisted in building an organ for the Swedish church near Philadelphia in 1713 and it is strongly probable that he built the one installed 1740 in the Gloria

---

[3] Louis E. Benson, *The English Hymn, Its Development and Use* (New York: George H. Doran, 1915), p. 185.

Dei church. In 1746 he built a positive organ for the Moravians in Bethlehem.

In 1745 Edward Bromfield, Jr., started building an organ in Boston, designed for 1,200 pipes, but died before its completion. We do not know whether it was ever completed or installed.

Thomas Johnston of Boston built organs in the 1750's. David Tanneberger came from Germany in 1749 and worked for a time with the Moravian organ-builder, Gottfried Klemm. Tanneberger is credited with building fourteen organs—the last in 1804 for the Lutheran church in York, Pennsylvania.

Gottfried Klemm was probably the most important builder of that era. In 1737 he built for Trinity Church in New York what would appear to be the first American-built organ—and a large one for its day, with three manuals and twenty-six stops.

OTHER INSTRUMENTS IN CHURCH

The shortage of church organs prompted the widespread use of other instruments, sometimes leading to almost disastrous results. Some people left the church because of it. Others walked out of the service when instruments were played.

The bass viol was among the first instruments to be used, but cello, flute, oboe, clarinet, and bassoon were also popular quite early. When the violin was introduced later, it met with strong opposition. Even the pitch-pipe had to be used on the sly during the latter part of the century. After organs became more numerous, the instrumentalists felt less needed, and the people were glad enough to do without them.

THE FIRST CHOIRS IN AMERICA

Church choirs began flourishing after the middle of the century, frequently as a result of singing-schools begun early in the century and conducted by itinerant musicians.

These traveling teachers lacked formal training in music and had gleaned most of their musical knowledge from what few textbooks were available at the time, which included Tansur's *Musical Grammar,* published in England; Thomas Walter's *The Grounds and Rules of Musick Explained,* Boston, 1721; and Fux's *Gradus ad Parnassum,* still a standard source today. The books served a dual purpose: (1) as sources of choral music and (2) as a means of learning music theory.

The singing-school sessions were held wherever convenient—in a home, a schoolhouse, a church, or even a tavern. The students paid a fee, the teacher's only renumeration except for what profit he might make on the books he sold them. Invariably these included some of his own—often crude—compositions. Class sessions took place one to five times a week, usually in the evenings, and a "term" could vary anywhere from six weeks to three months (or even longer). Since the teacher often used a bass viol in class, it came to be used in the churches as well.

The young people who attended these sessions often had other than musical motives. It gave them an opportunity, among other things, to get away from parental supervision and to be with those whose company they enjoyed—an incentive that dominates many a church choir member's participation even today!

Among the most illustrious of these early teachers was William Billings (1746-1800), a tanner by trade but with a certain adeptness in matters musical. His so-called "fuguing pieces" for choir were a rather weak imitation of contemporary European music, but considering the limitations of his training they are rather remarkable. He is also credited with introducing the pitch pipe and the cello to American choirs. Of the descriptions that several historians have provided us concerning the performance of his compositions, the following by Hubbard is fairly representative for our purposes:

> They are sung from beginning to end without any attempt at expression, each part trying to outdo the other in vigor and in volume. According to the custom of the time the air, then termed the tenor, and the bass were sung by the men; the true tenor part, which then was known as the treble was sung by the women, while the alto or counter was taken either by the men falsetto or by women and boys.[4]

Attempts to perform these compositions were not always appreciated nor understood by either the lay people or the clergy. After listening to the choir at one service, a minister was prompted to remark, "You must try again, for it is impossible to preach after such singing." [5]

Choirs became a rather common feature of American church life after the close of the Revolutionary War, but a number of churches continued to have only psalm-singing, and some did not permit even

---

[4] W. L. Hubbard, *History of American Music* (Toledo: Irving Squire, 1908), p. 159.
[5] *Ibid.*, p. 160.

this. In 1656 the First Baptist Church of Newport, Rhode Island, underwent a schism. Twenty-one of its members seceded and organized an "anti-singing" church, and this church held out against singing for more than a century. In 1765 the congregation voted by a narrow margin to sing one psalm at the beginning of each service. Those who objected remained outside the church until this "offensive exercise" was over.

While special seats were assigned to the choir, their only function at first was to "set the tune" and to lead the congregation in singing the psalms. Before long, however, they were beginning to contribute special selections of their own. Hymnbooks published in the second half of the century would frequently include a few anthems for the choir. Some churches were reluctant about having "special singers" in their midst; others forbade them entirely.

In 1779 the town of Worcester, Massachusetts, voted that the small group of singers who had been assisting in the service should constitute a choir and be placed in the front gallery, where they could more effectively lead the congregation in singing the psalms. They moved further to discontinue the services of the precentor. The office of the precentor was one of distinction, and a man who had enjoyed such status for many years was not easily pushed aside. The records show that

> the Sabbath succeeding the adoption of these votes, after the hymn had been read by the minister, the aged and venerable Deacon Chamberlain, unwilling to desert the custom of his fathers, rose and read the first line according to the usual practice. The singers, prepared to carry the alteration into effect, proceeded without pausing at the conclusion. The white-haired officer of the church, with the full power of his voice read on, until the louder notes of the collected body overpowered the attempt to resist the progress of improvement, and the deacon deeply mortified at the triumph of musical reformation, seized his hat, and retired from the meeting house in tears.[6]

In a Massachusetts church the precentor, after suffering the humiliation of hearing the choir lead the congregation in the psalm, patiently waited until it was finished, then said, with opened book and his spectacles down on his nose, "Now let the people of God sing."

While it was commonly necessary to import organists from Eng-

---

[6] George Hood, *A History of Music in New England* (Boston: Wilkins, Carter, 1846), p. 183.

land, the choir director was usually a local person who could be chosen from the congregation or brought in from the town. This meant that the latter often had relatively poor musical preparation, because of the meager opportunities in this country for the serious study of music. As the choir prepared to sing, the director would sound the keynote and then give the pitch for each part. The choirs often sang without music, relying on a number of songs they had learned while attending the singing schools.

As European music became more readily available toward the close of the century, the choral repertoire was greatly expanded and choral music gained in quality as well. How refreshing and challenging this music must have seemed in comparison with the poorly written compositions of the self-taught composers! This innovation also put an end to the singing schools, except in the southern part of the country, where they continued until about 1850. After the Revolutionary War a great number of European musicians came to this country, and the leadership formerly exercised by American-born musicians was soon taken over by these immigrants. On the other hand, those American students who studied under these Europeans soon realized that native American music was not quite up to European standards.

Not that early American composers were completely lacking in stature. One need only mention Francis Hopkinson (1737-91), William Billings (whom we have already met), and James Lyon (1735–94) who published *Urania,* a collection of psalm tunes, anthems, and hymns in settings of two, three, and four parts. There was also Josiah Flagg, publisher in 1764 of the first American book to have the music written out in four parts. His book contained only two anthems.

By the end of the century over 130 collections containing anthems had been published, with the word "anthem" frequently being a part of the book title, evidence of the growing popularity of special numbers sung by the choir.

In 1781 Andrew Law, a minister in Connecticut, printed an edition of Watts' *Psalms of David, Imitated,* in which he included sixteen pages of tunes printed with shaped notes—a system that assigned a different shape—square, diamond, circle, triangle, etc.—to each note of the scale. This system of notation had once been quite popular in England.

Two Protestant groups that settled in eighteenth-century America

116

have made notable contributions to choral music. The more colorful of these groups—who arrived in 1720 and founded a community known as the Ephrata Cloister in what is now Lancaster County, Pennsylvania—was a band of mystics under the leadership of Conrad Beissel and Peter Miller. The system of music these people promoted had an influence on German settlers over a comparatively large area, including New England and the region west of the Alleghenies, even though no one in the settlement was a really skilled musician.

Beissel established choirs and conducted singing schools throughout his community, wrote a *Dissertation on Harmony,* composed hymns, and played various instruments, including the violin. His choirs sang music in two, four, five, and seven parts, probably without accompaniment. His repertory included about 1,000 selections, most of them in four-part settings. One discipline imposed on choir members was the observance of certain dietary regulations. In fact, each section in the choir had its own special diet!

The second group of importance to American church music were the Moravians, who first settled in Georgia (1735) then moved on, five years later, to the Lehigh Valley of Pennsylvania. Moravian music was of a much higher level than that of the Ephrata group. In 1744 they formed the *Collegium Musicum,* a musical society that performed chamber music and symphonies by Europe's best composers. One of their members, Johann Peter (1746-1813), wrote several fine string quintets.

Later in the century a group of Moravians left Pennsylvania for what is now Winston-Salem, North Carolina. They built churches, installed organs, organized trombone choirs, and promoted various types of choral and instrumental music.

THE NINETEENTH CENTURY

ORGAN CONSTRUCTION AND PERFORMANCE

Since the early part of the nineteenth century, most of the organs used in American churches were built here, although at first by English-born craftsmen. The manufacture of reed organs, often called melodeons or harmoniums, began in 1818. Some of the larger models had two manuals and a pedalboard. The knee-operated swell was introduced in the second half of the century.

Mason and Hamlin (and later the Estey company) developed an improved system of voicing the reeds, which enabled their instruments to remain well in tune even under adverse climatic conditions. This made them especially desirable for smaller churches that remained unheated in winter except during the hours of worship.

Both organ-building and organ performance were of a decent quality by midcentury. A number of fine English organists had settled in the country by this time, but their influence seldom reached much beyond the churches they served.

As organs became more numerous, the use of other instruments waned. By 1850 the earlier shortage of organists was also partly remedied. In 1814 the Park Street church in Boston was still using an instrumental group—flute, bassoon, and bass viol—to accompany the singing. The Hanover Street church used clarinet, ophicleide (a large wind instrument of brass and copper), and a double bass as late as 1845, although some of its members had organs in their homes. Nathaniel Gould commented (1853, in his *Church Music in America*) that the first organ to be found west of the Allegheny Mountains was in the Second Presbyterian Church of Cincinnati, installed 1837.

In the early part of the century there was not an organ or an organist that could do justice to a Bach fugue. It remained for George W. Morgan, a brilliant young English organist who came to New York in 1853, to introduce Bach's organ music to America. Morgan was active first at Grace Church and later at the Brooklyn Tabernacle.

The organ was by no means universally accepted in this country. In churches where the organ was not fully accepted, the organist resorted to playing softly, so as not to be too conspicious. Before long, however, organists became bolder, and began to turn on the volume. Thus Nathaniel Gould stated in 1853 that

> many times now when the doxology is sung, at the close of worship, we hear such a crash of sound on the organ, that, the choir and the whole congregation joining could no more make words intelligible, than would be the words of a public speaker in the midst of roaring artillery.[7]

He complained also that organists played snatches of popular music, waltzes, marches, etc., "more unmeaning and flighty than the music of the street organ grinder."

Whereas the Presbyterians in Scotland had authorized the use of organs by the latter part of the century, their conservative coreligion-

---

[7] Nathaniel Duren Gould, *Church Music in America* (Boston: A. N. Johnson, 1853), pp. 179, 180.

ists the Reformed Presbyterian Church in America would permit neither organ nor choir in the service. The Orthodox Congregationalists and the New England Baptists had begun using the organ by about 1827. Wesley allowed an organ to be installed in the Bromfield Street Methodist Episcopal Church of Boston as a means of keeping the young people interested. In the latter half of the century there were some Presbyterian groups that permitted the organ, but the conservatives remained adamantly opposed to it.

In 1888 John L. Girardeau, a Presbyterian and an instructor at Columbia Theological Seminary in South Carolina, published a pamphlet, *Instrumental Music in Public Worship of the Church,* in which he supported the use of the organ. The 1884 General Assembly of the Presbyterian Church in the United States took no firm stand against the organ and even stated for the record that it favored each session's deciding such a "delicate and important matter," i.e., how to arrange and conduct the musical portions of the service.

How one American of the late nineteenth century felt about the organ performances can be seen from the following:

There were substantially three, or perhaps we might say four, ways of playing the organ. In one, the so-called legitimate or German method, the player deals largely with full organ, and carries an independent obligato melodic part with his feet, entirely distinct from that played by the left hand. This independence of the left hand from the feet, or the feet from the left hand, is the most arduous difficulty of legitimate organ technique. It is doubly difficult to the pupil of the present time, because it involves a new habit of music thinking, polyphonic, or many-voiced, instead of one-voiced, or melodic.

The second principal school is the English, less strongly developed upon the pedal side, but strong in registration, or the clever imitation of orchestral effects by means of the organ.

Then there is the French school, in which the right hand has a melodic part, the left hand an accompaniment, and the feet a pedal part consisting mainly of detached fundamentals. Great attention is paid in this school to orchestral coloring, or rather to contrasts of tone color.

Fourth, there is the American school, which in the olden times consisted in playing a few pleasing melodies upon fancy stops of impossible orchestral coloring, with pedal parts put in according to the French school.

The modern school of organ playing, as illustrated by the best virtuosi, consists of a combination of all these, having at command the fluent

119

technique of the German, the cleverness of the English, the piquancy of the French, and upon exhibition nights the old-time *ad captandum* methods of the unschooled organist of fifty years ago.[8]

The greatest American organist of the late 1800's and early twentieth century was Clarence Eddy, who concertized widely in Europe and America. His most phenomenal achievement was to present a series of one hundred recitals (every Saturday for two years) in Hershey Music Hall, Chicago, where he played over 500 compositions without once repeating any number.

CHORAL PERFORMANCE AND CHORAL MUSIC

The "fuguing pieces" with which numerous choirs were occupied toward the close of the eighteenth century had fallen into disuse by early in the nineteenth, probably because the standards in musical taste had risen enough to deprive such compositions of their appeal. The works of English composers, not favored hitherto, now became popular, adding considerably to the quality and quantity of choral music available.

One of the really fine church choirs of the early part of the century was that of Park Street Church in Boston, an organization of some fifty voices under the direction of Elnathan Duren. It had some of the best English anthems in its reportory, and was the nucleus around which the Handel and Haydn Society was later formed. At midcentury the singing of this organization was far superior to that of most contemporary choirs. They drew large audiences from all the denominations, including visitors from other cities. For instrumental accompaniment they used a combination of flute, bassoon, and cello.

A number of American choral composers made significant contributions early in the century. There was Thomas Hastings (1787-1872), composer of Toplady, to which "Rock of Ages" is usually sung; Nathaniel Gould (1781-1864), a Boston conductor and writer; Lowell Mason (1792-1872), often called the father of American church music, who wrote such well-known hymn tunes as Harwell (Glorious Things of Thee Are Spoken), Olivet (My Faith Looks up to Thee), and Hamburg (When I Survey the Wondrous Cross). In 1822 Mason's *The Boston Handel and Haydn Collection of Music,* published under the auspices of that society, included many

---

[8] Granville L. Howe, *A Hundred Years of Music in America* (Chicago: G. L. Howe, 1889), p. 236.

of his own compositions and some by European composers. For many years it was the main source of material for American church choirs and singing societies.

That these men had an uphill climb is evident from an address presented 1809 before the Handel Society of Dartmouth College by a certain Francis Brown:

> The greater part of those in our country who have undertaken to write music have been ignorant of its nature. Their pieces have little variety and little meaning.[9]

In evaluating the products of American composers and pointing out their weaknesses, he listed the following:

> First, the passion for novelty; second, the antipathy of the higher classes, more particularly of the ladies, to taking part in the music of the sanctuary; third, the lack of attention to the character and qualifications of the instructors.

About 1825 the American composers began moving the melody from the tenor to the soprano part, as Lukas Osiander had done in Germany (1586) and as had been common practice in Europe for two hundred years. (A favorite American hymn, Coronation [All Hail the Power of Jesus Name], was originally written with the melody in the tenor by Oliver Holden, who died in 1844.)

Removing the melody from the tenor met with considerable opposition in some quarters. Some said it was contrary to Scripture and that it interfered with the rights of men. Some felt that it was wrong because it gave women the leading part instead of the men. Even though Andrew Law had made this change in his *Select Harmony* (published 1778) and his *Collection of Best Tunes and Anthems* (1779) the practice was very slowly adopted.

The Oxford Movement, started in England in 1833, also had its followers in America. By midcentury a number of boy choirs were to be found in the American Episcopal churches, the first having been organized about 1839 by the Rev. Francis Hawks of St. Paul's College, Flushing, Long Island. Within six years Dr. William Augustus Muhlenberg had started a boy choir at the Church of the Holy Communion in New York, and before the century was over a number of boy choirs were in existence, some even in the Midwest. The peak of the boy choir movement was reached 1890-1910.

---

[9] W. L. Hubbard, *op. cit.*, p. 163.

121

Another feature of the Oxford Movement was the matter of surpliced choirs. Rev. Hawks wanted vestments in 1839 but had to forego this because of strong opposition. Dr. Muhlenberg's choir was not vested. Because of the opposition both to vestments and to the Choral Service the General Convention of the Episcopal Church adopted a motion in 1871 that forbade the rector to introduce the Choral Service without the permission of the vestry. Surpliced choirs were similarly restricted. If surplices were to be used, the directive specified that they should reach to the ankles.

Vested choirs were introduced to Boston about 1856 by Dr. Henry Cutler, but when he began work at Trinity Church in New York City, he found more opposition, and their use there had to be delayed. Only for some unusually auspicious event, such as the visit by the Prince of Wales to Trinity Church, was the wearing of vestments acceptable. But by the end of the century there were vested choirs of boys and men in most of the large cities, including Cincinnati, St. Louis, Chicago, San Francisco, Philadelphia, and Pittsburgh.

A third element of church music promoted by the Oxford Movement was the sung service, probably first performed by Dr. Muhlenberg's choir in New York. It also was firmly opposed in the beginning. The Church of the Advent in Boston introduced the Choral Eucharist shortly after its choir was established in 1852. By the mid-1890's, the sung service had been introduced into Episcopal churches in the area immediately west of Chicago. Canon J. H. Knowles, the first to lead such a service in this area, describes the occasion:

> After graduation I came back to Chicago and was detailed for duty at Aurora and Naperville. In the former place I presume the first Choral Service in the West was held on one wet Sunday morning, when not a soul came to church but myself, the quartette choir, the sexton and Mr. W. S. B. Matthews, the organist. He, ever eager for new knowledge, had got from me all the points on the Choral Service, so then and there we had a solemn function all by ourselves, the choir in the gallery, the parson in the chancel, the church empty (of all but angels) and the sexton looking wonderingly on.[10]

The "quartet choir," a fairly common phenomenon in church music circles by early in the century, consisted of a group of four soloists who usually sang as a quartet but sometimes joined in with the larger

---

[10] Granville L. Howe, *A Hundred Years of Music in America* (Chicago: G. L. Howe, 1889), p. 269.

volunteer choir. Some churches preferred the quartets to the volunteer choirs because of the latter's behavior in church. But one English cleric, after hearing a quartet, was not so impressed by this argument:

A female contralto voice murmering inarticulate utterances, sustained by an organ accompanient scarcely more audible than would have been the tones of a musical snuff-box heard at an equal distance. . . . Soon the organ put on a crescendo, and a soprano voice broke in with equally inarticulate utterances, which presently culminated in a blood-curdling shriek; a bass and a tenor by this time assisting in the performance which lasted about five minutes and concluded without conveying any single idea to my mind, except one I found to be in some degree sustained by fact—that I had been listening to very indifferent opera singers . . . the large congregation standing meekly while the four actors gayly disported themselves up and down the diatonic and chromatic scales.[11]

So far as deportment in church is concerned, the quartets were not without their faults. New York's *Musical Pioneer,* published the following story in June 1865:

In the country churches, where the members of the choir are usually members of the congregation, it is a rare thing for any individual of the singers to leave before the service is over; but among the singers in city churches, in the fashionable well-paid quartette, it is a frequent practice. In Episcopal churches particularly, where, in the morning service, no hymn is sung after the sermon, it is almost the rule for the choir to sneak out, one after the other, as soon as the text is given out. The soprano will first gather up her skirts, perhaps bend her head a little so as to avoid the notice of the congregation, and step gingerly out of the organ loft, not unfrequently, however, sweeping down a few books, or upsetting a chair, in spite of all her care. The basso, having no skirts to impede his progress, darts out a few minutes after, and makes no noise till he gets to the stairs, where, unless he takes the trouble to slide down on the balusters, his heavy boots are heard trampling down like the rumbling of distant thunder. The alto and tenor follow, unless, indeed, they prefer to remain and have a quiet little flirtation together during sermon time. The organist, having to play the concluding voluntary, groans inwardly because he is thus debarred the privilege of flight, but consoles himself and supports the tedium of 'the preached word' by stealing out to a neighbouring bar-room—there are plenty of these accessible on Sunday, by back doors, to the initiated—where he can snatch a sherry cobbler or a

---

[11] Archibald T. Davison, *Church Music—Illusion and Reality,* p. 46.

glass of lager, and be back in time to play the congregation out. This is what church musicians think is fulfilling their whole duty.[12]

There were also reports that suggest the organist did not always get back in time and that occasionally he was in too high spirits to conclude his work.

It is not our intention, however, to exonerate the volunteer choirs, who also had problems whiling away the moments when the minister was preaching. Following an English custom, the choir of that day was often shielded from the view of other worshipers by heavy curtains that could be opened or closed at will. The singers thus had opportunity to entertain themselves during the sermon with such pastimes as reading, sleeping, drawing pictures, or conversing softly. Says a writer in 1853:

> I recollect that one very warm Sabbath afternoon the singers had *water-melons* and *lemonade,* wherewith to console themselves; and it happened that one of the gentlemen, in handing a slice to a lady singer, overset the pitcher of lemonade. This might not have been of much consequence, had the floor of the organ loft been liquor tight. But there were many chinks in it, and the lemonade trickled through pretty freely down into the broad aisle, to the discomfiture of the rector, and such of his congregation as were wakeful enough to notice passing events.[13]

In the second half of the century a number of the larger Protestant Episcopal churches in this country started choir schools patterned after similar institutions in England. The emphasis was on boy choirs or choirs composed of men and boys. "Old Trinity" in New York, true to its reputation as a leader in church music matters, in 1839 started its first permanent choir, composed of boys, women, and men. Their choir school began in 1843 and by 1859 there were no women in the choir. The Cathedral of St. Peter and St. Paul in Chicago started a choir school about 1870, St. Paul's of Baltimore in 1873.

The rector in the American Episcopal church, like his counterpart in the church of England, was in complete control of musical activities. In 1891 the church took formal action in this matter, enjoining upon him not only the responsibility of selecting the organist but also the choir director, the anthems (if any) sung by the choir, and the tunes to which the hymns were to be sung. If the rector chose to

---

[12] James Begg, *op. cit.,* p. 130.
[13] Nathaniel Duren Gould, *op. cit.,* p. 118.

delegate some of these responsibilities to a music committee or other individuals, he was still held finally responsible for any infringement of church law.

The Presbyterian Church moved very cautiously in its introduction of choirs and musical instruments to the service. The General Assembly in 1867 agreed that

> the introduction of choirs or musical instruments can be justified only as they serve this end (of inspiring and expressing devotion) and aid or accompany sacred song; and no display of artistic skill, no delicacy of vocal training, no measure of musical ability, compensates for the violation, or even neglect, of the proprieties of divine worship.[14]

By the end of the century a new type of choral organization was making its appearance: the children's choir. The First Presbyterian Church, Flemington, New Jersey, is credited with being the first to organize such a group. Because the movement received its first impulse in the nonliturgical churches where there were responses to be sung, it became customary for the choir to be used for "special music." This practice was then carried over into more liturgical churches (such as the Lutheran) who began with children's choirs.

The prevalence of paid quartets in the larger and more prosperous churches during the second half of the century obviously had its effect upon the style of musical composition. Since each singer was a soloist, the selections used had to give each an opportunity to "perform."

The alternation of four-part harmony and solo passages— sometimes with a solo for every part in the same composition— became the accepted structure of a quartet "anthem." Harry Rowe Shelley and Dudley Buck became the most prominent American composers in this medium, which scarcely merits the name of church music. It was more of a sporting proposition, with soloists vying with one another to impress their "audience," as in a concert at the opera house, with the soloists singing *to* the worshipers instead of aiding them by means of their musical contributions to participate in the service.

The early twentieth-century revival of the "chorus choir" tended to displace the "quartet choir" and put most of the music of Dudley Buck and his associates in storage.

---

[14] *Manual of Presbyterian Law for Church Officers and Members* (Presbyterian Church in the United States of America, 1950), p. 109.

VII

The Twentieth Century

IN ENGLAND
REVITALIZATION

The twentieth century saw England regaining its place in the world of music, first through a group of less notable composers, such as Hubert Parry (1848-1918), C. V. Stanford (1852-1924), and C. H. Lloyd (1849-1919). Following these, and for some years contemporaneous with them, were stars of the first magnitude, including such as Edward Elgar (1857-1934), Gustav Holst (1874-1934), Ralph Vaughn Williams (1872-1958), Martin Shaw (1876-1958) and the English-born Canadian, Healey Willan (1880-   ). While recognized for their work in other areas as well, the last three in particular have made significant contributions to church music.

The need for continuing improvement and reform was particularly evident in the first quarter of the century. In 1910 church music practices were criticized for their commercialism and professionalism, for the lack of cooperation between clergy and musicians, and the tendency to sacrifice quality for glamor as a means of attracting new members for the church.

There were some also who treated church music as a matter of indifference, who

> hold that [music] is a distracting influence, which takes away our thoughts from the central fact of worship; who commit it rather grudgingly to a place in the outer courts, but are averse to giving it further recognition or encouragement.[1]

[1] Sir W. H. Hadow, *op. cit.*, p. 5.

126

Hadow does not specify whether he is referring to the clergy or the laity!

THE CHOIR

The grandeur and position of eminence accorded the cathedral choirs had passed before the turn of the century, going the way of all those elaborate music establishments that had formerly been maintained by the royal courts of Europe. Few cathedrals could any longer maintain a competent music force. Choirs of men and boys were to be found only in the very largest churches. The problem was twofold: (1) it was difficult to find adults to devote the time necessary for rehearsing and singing one or two services a day and (2) the boys who were particularly talented in music were given scholarships and shipped off to the large schools. By 1934 only three out of fifty cathedrals and collegiate churches had choirs that sang the Matins and Evensong daily: St. Paul's in London and the cathedrals of Lichfield and Wells. Whereas for most of the nineteenth century the Communion Service had been sung at least once a week, by 1938 this was occurring only once a month.

Choirs, on the other hand, have become much more numerous in the smaller parishes. This has been a characteristic pattern in the entire field of music: as democratic principles in government and in the affairs of daily life have been more thoroughly exercised, music has become more the possession of the common man and less the prerogative of royal courts and wealthy people. While today the cathedral organist may not be able to live on the salary he receives, nearly every church in England has its own choir, whose primary function is to lead the congregation and possibly to sing an anthem. While there is still a preference for boys' voices on the treble parts—especially the soprano —women are used where necessary, and it is quite often necessary. Boys' voices are not as frequently used in the smaller parishes.

The Oxford Movement, as we noted already, influenced music practices by moving the choir from the rear gallery to the chancel and by introducing the wearing of surplices. These practices have continued for the most part. In 1910 A. M. Richardson wrote:

> The mixed choir used to be in the west gallery, the surpliced choir is now placed in the chancel. The change has clearly been due, not so much to a desire to improve the music as to insure that the choir shall be in every sense of the word worshippers, robed in a similar way to

the clergy, standing with them before the people, and plainly and evidently joining with and assisting them in the offering of prayer and praise.[2]

Here are substantial arguments for those who feel that the choir should be in the chancel! In more recent times, however, choirs have been moving back to the west gallery, the conclusion being that this is, after all, the proper place for them.

That everything may not have been functioning as smoothly as it might is evident from the 1951 *Report of the Archbishops' Committee,* which suggests that the choir should be of "such a standard that it can be listened to without pain. But the congregations may well be asked to exercise a certain tolerance in this respect." [3]

THE ORGAN

By about 1925 most of the smaller churches in England had an organ of some type, either a harmonium, an American organ, or a small pipe organ. Organists prone to be carried away with the importance of their position were given a warning in 1909 when the Rev. Maurice Bell reminded organists that they were in the main responsible for the good or poor singing of both choir and congregation. The organist must remember, Bell says,

that he is to underlie the voices and not overlay them . . . that it is always just possible that the congregation may get weary of you and your instrument.[4]

The 1922 *Report of the Archbishops' Committee* stresses much the same point:

The function of the organ is to be an adornment and not a necessity. When it becomes a necessity it is in danger of ceasing to be an adornment.[5]

The 1951 *Report* seems to be more cognizant of the importance of the organist's contribution when it states that

the final assessment of the organist's work would be based upon his ability to weld together the singing of the congregation and choir.[6]

---

[2] A. Madeley Richardson, *Church Music* (London: Longmans, Green & Co., 1910), p. 57.
[3] *Music in Church* (Westminster: The Church Information Board, 1957).
[4] Maurice F. Bell, *The Arts of the Church: Church Music* (London: A. R. Mowbray, 1909), p. 1.
[5] *Music in Worship* (London: Central Board of Finance of the Church of England, 1922), p. 5.
[6] *Music in Church,* p. 43.

This committee suggests also that the organist may, in playing for the hymns, vary the harmony from what is written and introduce varieties of tone and dynamics appropriate to the changing mood of the text.

The committee suggests further that churches finding the purchase of a pipe organ financially impossible should get a grand piano rather than a harmonium or an American organ. "The tone of these instruments is both depressing and tiresome."

The Canon Law of the Church of England as published in 1947 charges the minister with full responsibility for the conduct of the music program of his church.

> It belongs to the Minister to direct when the organ shall be played and when it shall not be played, to decide what parts of the service shall be sung, and to choose all chants, hymns, anthems, and other settings, both the words and the music, with such assistance as he may see fit to employ from persons skilled in music and liturgy.

> It is the duty of the Minister to choose only such chants, hymns, anthems and other settings as are appropriate to the solemn act of worship and prayer in the House of God as well as to the congregation assembled for that purpose; and to banish all irreverence in the practice and in the performance of the same.[7]

Greater recognition and responsibility is given the choirmaster and organist in the following clause adopted 1949 by the Upper House of Convocation of Canterbury:

> Where there is an organist and choirmaster, the Minister shall pay due heed to his advice and assistance in the choosing of chants, hymns and anthems, and other settings, and in the ordering of the music of the church; but at all times the final responsibility in these matters rests with the Minister.[8]

Previous to the adoption of this statement there had been no official recognition of the duties of either organist or choirmaster.

CHURCH MUSIC ORGANIZATIONS

England today possesses a well-organized training program and professional organization for its organists and choirmasters. The organist today is encouraged to prepare himself by

---

[7] Sidney S. Campbell, *Music in the Church* (London: Dennis Dobson, 1951), p. 18.

[8] *Ibid.,* p. 18.

129

obtaining first-rate organ instruction
continuing his piano studies
preparing himself in sight-reading, transposition, score-playing, harmonization (at the keyboard and written)
playing chamber music with good string performers
singing alto, tenor, or bass in the best choir he can join

Specific requirements as set forth by the Archbishop's Committee include

Harmonizing a melody in simple ecclesiastical style; adding an accompaniment to a hymn tune; answer questions on choir training; write an essay on some topic in church music.

At the organ, harmonize a plainsong hymn melody, a melody in psalm-tune style, and a melody in chorale style. Improvise a short movement on a given theme.

THE ROYAL COLLEGE OF ORGANISTS

The first formal organization for church musicians in England was the Royal College of Organists, founded 1864. This is not a teaching institution, but a certifying body. In 1866 it commenced giving examinations leading to the Fellowship Diploma. In 1881 it introduced the Associate Diploma examination. Since 1924 it has also given examinations in choir-training.

In 1881 this organization held a conference for organists and organ builders for the purpose of standardizing such matters as organ-building and the performance of organ music. The report of this conference was a landmark in the history of organ-building in England.

A regular feature of the activities of the Royal College of Organists is to sponsor lectures at different places in both England and Scotland, with the general aim of improving the organist's contribution to the worship service.

THE CHURCH MUSIC SOCIETY

The Church Music Society was inaugurated in 1906, with its stated purpose being "to facilitate the selection and performance of the music which is most suitable for different occasions of divine worship, and for choirs of varying powers." The society publishes many short papers, a number of which are listed in the bibliography of this volume.[9]

---

[9] See Nos. 5, 18, 31, 38, 61, 64, 70, 114, 139, 163, 192, 200, and 201 in the bibliography.

It has also fulfilled an important function by reprinting older music of exceptional value and acting as an advisory agency in the creation of an informed public opinion in the area of church music. Besides laboring to make the more desirable out-of-print choral music available, the society periodically publishes selections by contemporary composers.

THE SCHOOL OF ENGLISH CHURCH MUSIC

In 1928 the educational activities of the Church Music Society were taken over by the School of English Church Music, established in December of the previous year. This organization serves the Anglican Church throughout the world, with branches in Australia, New Zealand, and South Africa. At the close of its first year there were 105 church choirs affiliated with this organization. By midcentury over 2,300 choirs belonged. The activities promoted by the School of English Church Music have included arranging for instructional gatherings for choirs, publishing a quarterly magazine with many helpful articles, and publishing lists of music recommended for church use.

The School of English Church Music does not confer diplomas, but in 1937 the Archbishop of Canterbury instituted his own Diploma in Church Music, for which examinations are given by the School of English Church Music. Candidates for this special diploma must first become Fellows of the Royal College of Organists and must earn the choir-training diploma issued by this agency.

THE ROYAL SCHOOL OF CHURCH MUSIC

The School of English Church Music became the Royal School of Church Music in 1945. Its stated purpose is "to encourage the study, practice, and improvement of music, speech, and such other matters as are relevant to the seemly conduct of the services of the Church." This school has also absorbed the duties previously carried on by the College of St. Nicholas, founded 1929 at Canterbury. (St. Nicolas had been a training center for church musicians, the only one of its kind in England.)

The Royal School of Church Music offers a three-year curriculum and recommends a one-year course as a desirable minimum. But it also holds short, intensive courses of a week or so, and over the school holidays it conducts week-long courses for choir boys from affiliated churches all over Britain. At the present time there are 7,250 choirs worldwide that are affiliated with the Royal School of Church Music, and it operates at full capacity every year with a total enrollment of 1,200 boys.

The concern which this institution has for church music is well stated in its 37th annual report (1964): "It is the view of the Council that the Church must in the very near future give very serious thought to the training and remuneration of its musicians if the standard of congregational as well as choir singing is to be maintained even at its present, often unsatisfactory, level." In order to reach as many as possible, the short courses conducted are not only for choristers, organists, and choirmasters but also for the clergy. Visits are also made periodically to the various theological colleges to hold conferences with the students and explain to them the program and services of the Royal School of Church Music. When these students become parish ministers they will then know what assistance is available to them in conducting their parish music program.

* * *

Non-established church groups in England have for the most part adopted the use of choirs and organs. In the early part of the century all Wesleyan Methodist churches, for example, had dropped their prejudices against organs and choirs. In 1934 this church body organized its own church music organization—The Methodist Church Music Society—whose purpose is the artistic improvement of music in English Methodist churches.

IN SCANDINAVIA

Church music reforms in Scandinavia, already under way toward the close of the last century, are continuing to develop, so that today the professional church musician's training is about comparable to that of a pastor. The better-trained organists and cantors prepare themselves at one of the nation's conservatories, often supplementing this with study in other countries, mainly Germany and England. A four-year conservatory course is needed to qualify for the best positions. The common practice in Scandinavia is that one person serve both as organist and as choir director.

Church music positions in Denmark and Norway are ranked according to personal qualifications. Musicians of the highest rank are eligible for positions in a cathedral or some other large or important church, which are frequently full-time occupations. In some other churches the top-rank organist is responsible for a certain number of hours per week—which could include giving private lessons—and his responsibilities may involve looking after other organists in his area.

The middle category of organists serve in large churches where they will in all likelihood be involved in teaching music privately or in a school besides the regular routine required by the church.

The lowest qualification gives the organist certification for positions in some of the smaller churches, where it is assumed that he will have secretarial or teaching duties in addition to his church music program. Many have a second job. There are, of course, a great number of organists in the smaller churches who do not qualify even for this lowest rating.

DENMARK

Chorale books have remained the favorite target of criticism all over Scandinavia. The one most widely used in Denmark was produced in 1901 by V. Bielefeldt and sold over 47,000 copies in the thirty years following its publication. A similar publication by Thomas Laub was issued in 1918, and has been well received, but with less popularity than the Bielefeldt volume. Both of these works did much to break church music loose from the sterile chorale arrangements of the last century. The emphasis now is more on rhythmic diversity.

In addition to preparing a chorale book, Thomas Laub also wrote two books in which he set forth numerous proposals for improving Danish church music. His *Dansk Kirkesang* was published in 1918 and *Musik og Kirke* two years later. Typical of his critical comments in the second volume is the following, which berates organists who have gotten into the habit of playing long preludes to hymns, particularly to the hymn following the sermon:

. . . Long, deeply felt meditations upon the moving address just heard—well, maybe it had been heard and maybe it hadn't! A worshiper attending the service might ask, quite legitimately: "Why can't we get right on with the hymn? Why this interruption?" [10]

By the second decade of our century there were pastors, congregations, and organists in Denmark who saw that the role of church music

---

[10] Thomas Laub, *Musik og Kirke* (Copenhagen: Nordisk Forlag, 1920), p. 171.

would have to be reevaluated. They began stressing the need for more emphasis on church music education for the clergy and the organists, and a fresh look at the role of the church choir in worship.

Denmark's church music organization arranges two- or three-day meetings twice annually, and there are certain prerogatives that an organist can and does exercise. He may, for instance, refuse to play certain songs at weddings if he does not deem that the text or the music is of suitable quality.

Probably Denmark's greatest contribution to church music in the past quarter-century has been in the area of organ-building. The tonal quality and workmanship of the better Danish instruments is scarcely rivaled anywhere else in the world. Almost every Danish church now has a pipe organ.

Most of the churches in Denmark also have a choir. The larger churches have small paid choirs (Roskilde Cathedral has 10-12 members, all paid) augmented for festive occasions with volunteers. The choir usually sings four-part settings of the Introits all year long, occasionally adding a motet. Smaller churches may also have anywhere from three to ten professional singers, while many Danish churches have volunteer choirs composed of children and young people. The church music organization sponsors annual get-togethers for choir members, lasting as long as six days, a practice that helps generate a degree of interest in choral activities.

ICELAND

A little later getting started with its music program, Iceland has made considerable progress in the present century. The earlier chorale books have been replaced by one prepared in 1936 by Sigfus Einarsson and Páll Isólfsson. It is still in use. In recent years a committee has been at work preparing a new hymnal, to be followed by a companion chorale book for use by the organist. Many well-trained organists are to be found in Iceland today, most of them having taken studies at the Reykjavik Conservatory, in some cases supplemented by further study abroad.

Since about 1950 quite a number of organs have been installed in place of the harmoniums used previously. The organs are for the most part being imported from Denmark, Germany, England, and Czechoslovakia.

Organists in the Icelandic hinterland get a good deal of assistance and encouragement from church music headquarters. Teachers at the Reykjavik Conservatory—most of whom are church organists themselves—make short rural tours to conduct training sessions, and these contacts enable even those in the more remote areas to keep abreast of developments elsewhere.

Part-music has been readily—though belatedly—accepted by Icelandic singers, and owes its introduction to the journeys of a "song inspector" who stumped the country to organize and train choral groups. Church choirs have also received considerable assistance from church music organizations, whose purpose is to improve church music standards and to encourage the adequate training of leaders.

Where choirs exist, the Introit is often sung antiphonally by the pastor and choir, and the choir setting is in four parts. The children's choir movement has not made much progress in Iceland as yet. The larger centers feature choir and organ concerts in which the choir sings cantatas, motets, or—in some instances—major oratorios.

FINLAND

Finland first won world prominence in music in the early twentieth century, mainly through the outstanding compositions of Jan Sibelius, born in 1865. Since Finland belonged politically to Sweden for seven centuries prior to 1809 and to Russia from that date until 1919, it is only since the close of the First World War that the Finns have been free to develop an independent national culture. The first Finnish-language secondary school was not founded until 1858.

Lutheranism was introduced in 1528 under King Gustavus Vasa of Sweden, but Gregorian traits are evident in Finnish church music to this very day.

Musical activities and interests were multiplying by the late 18th century. The city of Turku, at one time the Finnish capital, had amateur orchestral, choral, and chamber music activities by 1790. The national university at Turku, burned with the rest of the city in 1827, was moved to Helsinki, the new capital, in 1828. Subsequently a department of music was inaugurated at Helsinki University, and by the early nineteenth century the University Music Society was sponsoring both instrumental and choral activities. Throughout that century, however, most of Finland's professional musicians were of alien— chiefly German—origin.

When Richard Faltin (1835-1918), a German, became head of

the Helsinki University music department, the cause of church music was given new impetus. As organist in what is now the Helsinki Cathedral and as a composer of choral music, he did much to acquaint the Finns with J. S. Bach's music.

Through a system of schools and private teachers the musical culture of Finland has penetrated even to the remote woodland areas. Superlative choruses are found throughout the country, and there are song festivals that attract considerable attention.

Almost all the contemporary Finnish churches have choirs. The smaller ones usually have a cantor in charge of the music program; larger ones divide the work between the cantor (in charge of choral activities) and the organist. Some of the larger churches operate a multiple-choir program consisting of two, three, or as many as five choirs. Children's choirs are scarce as yet, but the Helsinki Cathedral boy choir, founded 1953, won the BBC European boy choir competition in 1965.

How seriously the Finns take their church music is evident from the program of the Viipuri conservatory, which is concerned chiefly with instruction in church music and the preparation of church musicians. It is also to be seen in the fact that Finnish-built organs are in great demand.

NORWAY

Choirs have never played an important or consistent role in Norwegian churches since the Reformation period. In some cities there are groups that sing church music, but they are not affiliated with any specific congregation. A number of male choruses are also to be found throughout the country. For special occasions these groups may be asked to take part in the worship service, or a volunteer choir may be organized specifically for the event. About one hundred choirs (with a total enrollment of about 3,000 members) are now affiliated with *Norges Kirkesangforbund,* the national church music organization.

Churches that have no choir will frequently use a group of four to six singers (mostly women, with now and then a man or two included) to lead the congregation in singing the hymns and liturgical responses. Such singers are paid on an individual basis, while the established church choirs are paid as an organization. In some communities, children's choirs and boy choirs have been used successfully, and the idea has been promoted by national conventions.

The church choir situation in Norway might best be illustrated by what is being done in Trondheim and Bergen, two of the nation's largest cities. The Nidaros Cathedral in Trondheim has both a cathedral choir, which sings at all services, and a boy choir, which sings once a month. The cathedral organist also directs the *Olavskoret,* an independent organization that has close ties with the cathedral. Since 1937 the *Olavskoret* has given an annual performance of Bach's *Christmas Oratorio* and (at Easter) Bach's *St. John Passion.*

The Vår Frue church, also in Trondheim, has an oratorio choir that, besides singing at services, has given several performances of Handel's *The Messiah.* Neither the Nidaros Cathedral choir nor the Vår Frue oratorio choir participate *in toto* at every church service, but are represented from Sunday to Sunday by smaller groups.

Lademoen Church, Trondheim, has a boy choir and a motet choir. Other churches in this city also have choirs that participate regularly in the worship services, justifying Trondheim's claim to being the church-music center of Norway.

By contrast, not one of the seven state-supported (Lutheran) churches in the city of Bergen has a choir. Johanneskirke has five double quartets that take turns singing at the worship services. These participate in singing the liturgy and contribute a chorale or short anthem.

Ludwig Lindeman's chorale book, published 1871, remained the authorized book for Norwegian organists until the publication in 1926 of *Koralbok for den Norske Kirke,* which features Norwegian religious folk tunes and some new settings composed especially for this work. It was revised in 1936.

SWEDEN

Sweden's first twentieth-century chorale book was G. T. Lundblad's *Swedish Chorale Book in Revised Rhythmic Form,* published 1901. In his preface Lundblad says he felt something needed to be done to free Swedish hymn melodies from their "century-old shackles and assist them to a new rhythmical and naturally lively beauty." In 1916 the Lutheran Church in Sweden selected a committee to prepare a new chorale book, which was published 1921 but did not entirely satisfy the advocates of "rhythmical beauty." A supplementary collection, issued 1934, sought to meet this criticism.

Examinations are taken by the church organists in Sweden for the various levels of attainment. A number of organists are in full-time positions, although in some instances this may include giving private lessons. Those not assigned to the largest churches are generally teachers in the nation's school system.

Throughout the nineteenth century there was a dearth of choral activity. By the early part of the present century the tendency was for singers to be organized into municipal choirs that sometimes participated in church services. But as the century progressed, the movement toward church choirs gained considerable momentum, and most churches now have choirs of their own. Since 1950 all Swedish church musicians have been urged to train and direct church choirs, and a recent report states that Sweden has 2,000 church choirs with a total membership of 40,000 members. The choirs are volunteer organizations in the smaller communities but in the larger centers the choir members are paid.

Since mid-century there has been a large increase of choirs for children and young people, the present enrollment standing at about 15,000 members. Some churches have three or four choirs, so that there is something for every age group. The youth-choir movement deserves some credit for the relatively high percentage of young people that are now active church members. In recent years it has been a popular practice to have the adult choirs alternate with the congregation in singing hymns: a stanza by the congregation in unison, another by the choir singing in parts.

Church music activities during the past thirty years have also included numerous studies in liturgy and church music history. Several of Sweden's more talented composers have written choral music, and the larger choirs frequently perform cantatas, oratorios, and other large works with orchestral accompaniment. There are no less than ten reputable organ manufacturers within the borders of a country whose geographical area is slightly larger than that of Montana.

New developments in church architecture recognize the musical centrality of the choir, which means that not infrequently it sits in a traditional chancel-choir arrangement but is located in the transept. Some have suggested placing the choir in front of the congregation, facing the altar. Since the choir director and the organist are generally one and the same person, the organ will need to be near the choir. The organist usually has a *Rückpositiv* to shield him from the view of the congregation.

CHURCH MUSIC ORGANIZATIONS

Nearly all the organists and choirs of the five Scandinavian countries belong to some national church music organization, whose responsibility it is to give assistance to members and to provide a sense of direction for the total church music program. Members also receive informative periodicals designed to promote a steady growth in matters musical.

In Denmark no directives are likely to be issued by the church music office, but limits are suggested within which the work should be conducted on the congregational level. In Finland, Norway, and Sweden some directives have been given, such as to request that no solos be used in the worship services unless these appear as part of a selection by the choir.

They also arrange the get-togethers for choirs and organists. Sweden has been particularly successful with its choir conventions. One such meeting in Göteborg (in 1960) was attended by 4,000 singers.

There is also an annual Scandinavian Church Music Convention, sponsored by all five countries. There is no real language problem here, since the Norwegians, Swedes, and Danes normally converse with each other, while Swedish and Norwegian are a "second language" of the Finns and Icelanders respectively.

IN CONTINENTAL LUTHERAN CHURCHES

CHURCH MUSIC ORGANIZATIONS IN GERMANY

German church music received an impulse toward reform as early as 1829, when the *Berliner Gesangbuch* was published, but little real progress was made throughout the nineteenth century. As late as 1885 only a few choirs were functioning, and the organists of that era lacked an understanding of liturgical values. Toward the end of the century a number of churches were organizing volunteer choirs, regarded as a great improvement over the student-manned "town choirs," although there are a few of these around even today. Volunteer choirs were not new on the German scene. Some had been organized shortly after the death of J. S. Bach, but were not permitted at the time to participate in worship services.

The progress made by church music in twentieth-century Germany can be attributed to its church music organizations, which have done much to put the musician's work on a professional level. Toward the end of the nineteenth century a movement was already under way to set up a training program and a system of examinations for church music positions. It was sponsored jointly by the Lutheran and Catholic churches and by the government. In 1914 Karl Straube of the Leipzig Conservatory faculty attempted to launch a church music institute in the *Landeskirche* of Saxony, but World War I delayed the implementation of his program, so that the first examinations were not given until 1925.

In 1933 the Lutherans set up their own special schools for training church musicians, one for each *Landeskirche*. During World War II this program was in disfavor with the government because the schools were regarded as anti-Nazi propaganda centers, but after the war they were reactivated.

The training program of these music schools can lead to one of three classifications: A, B, or C, which serve as a guide to congregations seeking the services of a church musician.

The top classification (A) qualifies one to accept the very best positions. It is a professional rank that requires university training beyond that afforded by the church music school. To attain such a rating the organist must be able to

—play the main part of the service by memory, which includes supplying appropriate harmonizations for the various liturgical responses and settings and for the hymns
—transpose into any key
—improvise preludes to chorales
—perform satisfactorily the more difficult organ compositions from the baroque and contemporary periods
—perform standard piano literature, including Beethoven sonatas, selections by such composers as Debussy, Hindemith, and Stravinsky
—compose (on paper) chorale preludes and larger compositions for choir, soloists, organ, and orchestra
—read open score, each staff in the C clef

Since churches usually prefer one person to serve both as organist and as choir director, he must also

—sing a major work by Schütz or Buxtehude
—be familiar with vocal technique as applied to choral work
—demonstrate competency in handling various types of music suitable for social occasions at church gatherings
—conduct choral compositions, beginning with those of J. S. Bach and including those of contemporary composers

There are not many A-classification musicians in any one city. Brunswick, for example, with a quarter million inhabitants, has only three.

The B classification qualifies a musician for the smaller city positions, where they will not necessarily be employed on a full-time basis. Two or three years' training is required to meet its standards. While the B-examination is not as extensive nor as demanding as for the A classification, a substantial amount of very careful preparation is necessary. There are approximately six times as many B-musicians as those with the A-rating. A city like Helmstedt, with 30,000 inhabitants, has three with a B-rating, while two others hold C and D [11] classifications.

The C-examination qualifies a musician for work in a smaller community where the church music program will not be his main occupation. Such a person may also serve as a church secretary or a teacher of religion, or he may have other responsibilities besides those that involve the congregation's music program. The equivalent of one or two years in the music school are necessary to meet the requirements of the C classification, but some prepare for the examination without formally attending a school.

When the musician completes a specified course of training and has passed an examination, this does not mark the end of his professional training, especially if he does not hold an A classification. The *Landeskirchenmusikdirektor*—who may or may not be the area's cathedral organist—keeps in close contact with all the organists in his district, which could include as many as 120 churches. Every year or two—and this requires following a rigid schedule—he will visit all the organists in the larger population centers and at less frequent intervals those in the smaller communities. Besides this there are regular conventions held for all the organists. This type of inservice training will obviously insure a high standard of performance.

To coordinate all this activity at the national level is the task of the Society for Evangelical Church Choirs in Germany,[12] with which nearly all German Lutheran church choirs are affiliated. The Society furnishes its members with recommended lists of organ and choral

---

[11] The D classification is administered only in the Hannover and Brunswick *Landeskirchen,* both in northern Germany. Two thirds of the congregations in Germany have organists who do not hold as much as a D-rating.

[12] The *Christliche Sängerbund* performs the same function for the smaller Protestant groups.

compositions for every level of proficiency. It publishes a periodical with articles relating to the church musician's work. It advises as to what music should be used and what should be avoided. In Germany, for instance, it would be unthinkable to use either Wagner's or Mendelssohn's wedding march—compositions whose use has become a rather baneful adjunct to the ceremony in America.

Each Lutheran choir holds membership in its own *Landesverband,* which may have subsidiary organizations, corresponding to geographical subdivisions of the *Land,* or may, like the Bavarian *Verband,* be just one large organization. Each *Landesverband* sponsors its own conventions. Lower Saxony, for example, has a general convention for all its choirs every two years, and on the alternate years has area conventions representing the smaller geographical subdivisions. The 1966 general convention, held in Brunswick, was attended by 2,400 singers.

Besides the conventions there are numerous *Singwoche,* weekend sessions usually held in rural boarding houses operated by the church.

Choirs for youth and children are fairly common in Germany. The following recent report from Hamburg *Landeskirche* would seem to indicate a trend in total choir membership: [13]

Number of Members

	Children Up to Age 14	Ages 14 to 21	Over 21	Total
1962	1956	1159	1610	4725
1963	1683	1258	1576	4517
1964	1770	1223	1725	4718
1965	1657	923	1701	4218

MINORITY LUTHERAN BODIES

The Lutherans of Netherlands, France, Austria, and Switzerland are decidedly minority groups. Whereas the Lutheran Church of Austria has a church music organization similar to that of Germany, there are only about two Lutheran professional church musicians in the whole country. But as small and as few and as scattered as the Austrian Lutheran churches are, they manage to sponsor a *Singwoche* every summer, and the affair is always a success. Of the above-

---

[13] "Beunruhigende Statistik?" *Der Kirchenchor,* No. 2 (March–April, 1966), p. 29.

mentioned countries, the Dutch Lutheran Church has been the most progressive, even though it comprises only sixty congregations and no more than 60,000 adherents.

In 1942 the *Vereniging voor Protestantse Kerkmuziek* was organized as a joint venture of Reformed and Lutheran churches in the Netherlands. It has published Bach cantatas with Dutch texts and some early choral works by Dutch composers—notably Sweelinck—with the original French texts translated into Dutch. The efforts of Lutherans to have closer contacts with their coreligionists in other countries, particularly Germany, led to the founding of the Lutheran Working Group for Church Music, which arranges for choral festivals and workshops, edits choral music, and publishes *Musica Sacra,* a magazine for church musicians. The influence of this organization is felt even in the Dutch Reformed churches, which are now adopting some of the Lutheran musical traditions. Until the present century there were no church choirs in either the Lutheran or the Reformed churches of the Netherlands.

In 1962 a special church music program was instituted at the Dutch conservatories as a means of training church musicians for all the church bodies active in the country. Students who are admitted to these institutions may pursue a four-year course that leads to a certification approximating the German B-rating.

Most of the Lutheran churches in Holland, France, Austria, and Switzerland now have church choirs, but Lutherans in the latter two countries are of such small numbers that they cannot carry on a very highly developed church music program.

But the impact of Lutheran church music organizations in these countries is of enough depth that in 1955 the first International Lutheran Congress for Church Music was held in Amsterdam, Holland. European church music in general was given new impetus during the second quarter of this century by a revival of the liturgical concept of music in worship and by the contributions of several leading composers whose work is conceived along these lines.

IN THE REFORMED CHURCHES

The history of twentieth-century church music in the Reformed tradition focuses mainly on Scotland, Switzerland, and the Netherlands. The Evangelical Reformed Church of northwestern Germany, though a small church body, maintains a church music organization of its own (just over fifty choirs belong at the moment) whose main function is to promote congregational singing. Musically their achievements cannot be classified as "high level." Of much better quality is the work of the Rhineland denomination known as the United Church, whose membership stems from both Reformed and Lutheran elements.

By the middle of the century most of the churches of every denomination in Scotland had organs, although some still use other types of instrumental music. The choir movement got under way at the end of the last century and has been making steady progress. Early in the twentieth century the Church of Scotland issued a new *Church Anthem Book,* while by 1932 surpliced choirs were becoming more numerous and encouragement was being given to junior choirs.

The Dutch Reformed churches, for their part, were never very enthusiastic about church music and still show little interest, even today. Since 1650 the organist has been officially permitted to accompany congregational singing and in many cases to introduce the psalm-singing with short preludes, a method favored by Constantin Huygens, who felt that the organ should be used as a liturgical instrument.

Only recently has the idea of a church choir become of interest to the Dutch Reformed churches, and only a few have choirs. The choirs that actually function are used to sing settings of the Introits, nineteenth-century choral compositions, or four-part settings of hymns. Often they are thought of merely as a medium for teaching new hymns to the congregation. Musically they do not perform at a very high level.

The church choir movement in Switzerland has been a little more progressive. By the end of the last century there was a definite movement under way, and in 1898 Heinrich Weber founded the Swiss *Kirchengesangsbund* for Reformed church choirs of German background, which consisted at first of a few choirs in Zürich and eastern Switzerland. Today there are 447 church choirs, 15 youth choirs, and two *Posaunenchöre* (trombone choirs) enrolled, with a total membership of over 17,500.

About half the Swiss Protestant congregations now have choirs, but in some areas the ratio of choirs to congregations is very small. It is fairly common for choirs not affiliated with any church to sing for an occasional worship service. As with the Dutch Reformed choirs, much of their repertory—up to 90%—consists of hymns. The youth choir movement has made little headway in Switzerland thus far, but interest is growing. The younger group participates in the worship service in the same manner as an adult choir.

The effects of the liturgical revival in Germany after World War II have been felt in Switzerland as well, and reforms have been instituted. The more discerning (but not all) churchmen have discarded the old concept that choir and organ are meant only to "beautify" the service and are therefore "irrelevant."

Since the sixteenth century the Swiss Reformed Church has slowly been accepting the use of the organ. By 1940 they were generally found in those churches tracing their origins to Zwingli. Today some smaller churches in the hills and rural areas may have only a harmonium but are rapidly obtaining organs. In fact, it has become almost a prestige symbol to own a really fine organ. The present prosperity has permitted the churches to buy organs, and the factories are operating up to eight years ahead of their delivery schedule. Many of the new organs are replacing earlier instruments that have not stood the test of time.

IN BRAZIL

It is encouraging to know that in Brazil, where Protestantism is a small minority, there is a dedicated and determined band of church musicians in action. The School of Sacred Music, which trains church musicians, was established in 1937 at Colégio Bennett. The Independent Baptists and the Presbyterians also operate music schools.

The church music program is largely choral, since as yet the costs of carrying on a fully-developed program in organ music is too great for the resources available. Most churches in the interior have a harmonium or a piano, although the accordion and guitar are also used in the smaller, more isolated areas. The high cost of pipe organs—but also the climate and the termites—has discouraged their use, but some electronic instruments are being employed.

IN CANADA

Choral societies have existed in Canada since the latter part of the eighteenth century, but their activities were considerably stepped up during the early nineteenth, so that by midcentury a number of groups had performed major choral works with orchestral accompaniment.

145

The trend continued into the twentieth century, and Toronto, with its five large choral groups, lays claim to being the choral capital of North America. By the present century almost every town had a church choir, and the larger cities have some of the best to be found. Dr. Healey Willan of Toronto, besides being one of the century's outstanding choral composers, also maintains an excellent choir.

By midcentury a considerable variety of choral music was being used in the churches: works of early English composers such as Tye, Tallis, Weelkes, Gibbons, and (to a lesser degree) William Byrd; compositions by Croft, Purcell, Greene, and S. S. Wesley; and somewhat poorer offerings by such nineteenth-century composers as Stainer and Barnby. Contemporary works include such material as the works of Healey Willan, Martin Shaw, and Charles Wood. And in the past few decades the music of J. S. Bach has become better known.

A number of the Anglican churches of Canada are affiliated with the Royal School of Church Music in England, and these have many high-quality choirs. There are some choirs composed of both boys and men, but the more common pattern in the larger churches is to have a mixed choir, a paid quartet, and a boys' group.

The United Church of Canada, organized in 1925 from former Presbyterian, Congregational, and Methodist congregations, has given special promotion to the use of chancel choirs. A group of Presbyterian congregations that did not go along with the merger—now known as the Presbyterian Church in Canada—have also made significant contributions to church music. Some of their church choirs have sung a number of the Bach cantatas and Handel oratorios, sometimes with orchestral accompaniment. One of their Ottawa choirs gives an annual performance of Bach's *St. Matthew Passion.*

Some Canadian Baptists tend to be quite liturgical. They have choir processionals, and the choir sings the Introit and other portions of the liturgical service. Other Baptists are quite the opposite, and these often have questionable standards in music, with some steps toward improvement in the last decade.

In Canadian Lutheran churches the choir customarily sings the Introit and the Gradual and leads the congregation in other parts of the liturgical service.

While church choirs and choral societies of various types have made enviable progress in Canada, not as much can be said for their organists. There are a number of very fine organs and organ-builders—the

Casavant Company began its work in 1837—but the training of organists is far below United States standards.

The Royal Canadian College of Organists, founded in 1909 along the general lines of the Royal College of Organists in England, has been particularly successful in setting church music standards, and through its conventions it has given the organist a sense of professional status. The RCCO has eighteen examining centers across Canada, but only a handful of organists present themselves for the examination.

Summer sessions in church music are conducted at the Royal Conservatory of Music in Toronto, at the London (Ontario) School of Church Music, and elsewhere.

IN THE UNITED STATES

DEVELOPMENTS IN OUR TIME

In tracing the fortunes and misfortunes of church music from the early sixteenth century up to the beginning of the twentieth, we can see that reform measures initiated toward the end of the last century have not yet reached their fulfillment, even today. Besides the reforms that seemed desirable three quarters of a century ago, there are other changes that would seem relevant to our disengagement from the sentimental and emotionally charged elements of the Romantic period, which provided the original impetus for reform.

Two twentieth-century Americans have distinguished themselves in this latter area of reform: Waldo Selden Pratt (1857-1939) pointed the way for needed changes in his *Musical Ministries in the Church,* (1901), a book that enjoyed a healthy circulation, reaching its fifth edition in 1923. Peter C. Lutkin (1858-1931), who established a Department of Church Music at Northwestern University just before the turn of the century, was in a unique position to influence many university music students. As a composer of church music, a conductor, a lecturer, and an author, he also reached thousands of people beyond the bounds of the university campus. His *Music in the Church* (1910) embodied a number of ideas that have since been put into practice.

Publications such as these, together with the nationwide activities of the American Guild of Organists, were powerful forces during the first half of the century in setting the pace for American church music.

One needs only to hear some of the organs built thirty to fifty years ago to realize that the concept of appropriate worship music has changed since then. The mushy-voiced "orchestral" instrument of the early twentieth century was not appropriate for use in church. As recently as 1933, Archibald Davison was led to lament that

> the church has of late years cultivated a type of organ which exploits the percussion devices of the orchestra, such as the celesta, which suggests fairy bells, the harp, and the chimes.[14]

A revival of baroque principles in organ construction and organ music performance, begun about 1925, has dominated the scene ever since. It was instigated by German organ builders, who had for their models the famous seventeenth- and eighteenth-century organs built by Schnitger and Silbermann. Other builders were soon to follow their example, notably the Englishman Emerson L. Richards and the Americans Walter Holtkamp and G. Donald Harrison. (Danish builders such as Marcussen and Frobenius began their work just after World War II.)

In this country it was Walter Holtkamp who introduced the baroque revival by building a demonstration organ for the 1933 convention of the American Guild of Organists, whose efforts since then have been particularly effective in reestablishing the baroque traditions. In 1935 Harrison also built an organ similar to that of Holtkamp for the Groton School Chapel. His work has influenced American organ builders ever since.

The characteristic features of the more recent American organs are not confined to mechanical items—low wind-pressure, new tonal colors in the reed, flute, string, and French horn stops, an increased number of couplers—but include a wide range of mixtures and mutations that provide the organist with more subtle color variations.

Some firms in England have revived a much earlier practice of building two great organs instead of a great and a choir, which makes possible the proper rendition of Bach compositions and the works of contemporary German composers. Some of the largest German organs today have only a small number of pistons, but in gadget-conscious America these have become a prominent feature of organ-building.

Electronic instruments were first developed in France in 1930 by Messrs. Compleux and Givelet. In 1935 the first American electronic instrument was marketed by Laurens Hammond. The Everett company introduced their Orgatron the same year. Different methods have

---

[14] Davison, *Protestant Church Music in America*, p. 158.

been used to generate the tone, but all electronic instruments depend upon electrical amplification for their volume.

AMERICAN CHOIRS

Organ construction and organ music are not the only areas of change on the American scene. Considering that J. S. Bach's choral music was practically unknown in America until the Bethlehem Bach Choir inaugurated its Bach festivals in 1912, there has obviously been a development in the area of choral music.

Two church music training centers that have exerted a nationwide influence were established early in the twentieth century: the Westminster Choir College (1926) and the School of Sacred Music at Union Theological Seminary (1928). Since then a number of colleges have introduced special curricula for church musicians, and a number of state universities now offer graduate degrees in this area of study.

CHURCH MUSIC ORGANIZATIONS

One of the most encouraging developments in contemporary American church music has been the concern shown by numerous church bodies for the propagation of good music in their churches. In the early 1920's the Methodists instigated several changes inspired by a series of three special conferences held in Indiana. The Methodist music reformers of that era must have faced a staggering task. As Richard L. Cannon stated in 1921, "The Methodists have been the bitterest opponents of classic church music." [15]

The Southern Baptists began studying their church music in 1937, and steps for improvement were initiated shortly thereafter. They have been particularly successful with their multiple-choir program. The Protestant Episcopal Church set up a commission on church music in 1919, and in 1925 the Presbyterian Church appointed a commission on music and worship. These activities resulted eventually in the formation of permanent church music organizations which are becoming increasingly important in molding and guiding the church music program on the congregational level.

---

[15] Richard L. Cannon, *Defense of Classic Church Music* (Cincinnati: Methodist Book Concern, 1921).

a. The American Guild of Organists

Founded in 1896 and chartered by the Board of Regents of the State of New York, the AGO is an association to which all organists may belong. It is not a training center but an examining body. Its' better than 17,000 members belong to 280 chapters and branches throughout the United States and the Panama Canal Zone, and it publishes a quarterly periodical and numerous pamphlets on various aspects of church music. For many years *The Diapason* was the official magazine for both the American Guild of Organists and the Royal Canadian College of Organists. Since October 1967, the former started issuing its own publication: *Music, the A.G.O. Magazine.*

The Guild has three types of membership by examination: Fellowship, Associate, and Choir Master. A recent report states that 402 hold membership in the first category, 1,418 in the second, and 205 in the third.

b. The Church Music Department of the Southern Baptist Convention

The Southern Baptist Convention, acting through its Sunday School Board, established a church music department in 1944, as the culmination of a movement that began in 1937, when a committee was appointed to consider how a music program might be inaugurated. It was in 1937 that the Convention of the Church accepted the following statement in a report: "We would again call the attention of our churches to the added necessity for more serious and adequate concern relative to the place and standards of music and verse in the worship of God."

The 1944 Convention accepted the recommendation that "we urge our Baptist colleges, universities, and seminaries to place in their curriculum a Department of Church Music and that certain definite courses be required of all ministerial students." It was in this year that the Church Music Department was officially launched. At the present time, thirty-five of the thirty-seven senior colleges of the Southern Baptist Convention offer a degree in some area of music. Twenty offer a degree in Church Music.

The Church Music Training Course was developed in 1946, with approved programs leading to two graded diplomas. The Church Music Department conducts churchwide conferences each year, the first of which was held in 1940. The two one-week conferences held in

1964 were attended by approximately 5,000 church musicians. Classes are held for choir directors, professional classes for the experienced directors, instruction in piano, voice, organ, music theory, hymnology, graded choirs, etc. The week-long session usually closes with the presentation of a major oratorio, such as *The Messiah* or *Elijah.*

One basic principle of the Church Music Department is that the music program of the church should be conducted on the same level as the Sunday school and other areas of major concern. Its publications are disseminated in all fifty states and in several foreign countries, and twenty-eight states now have full-time church music secretaries who promote the music program and assist the congregations in establishing, conducting, improving, and enlarging the ministry of music in the church. Some states also have a full-time associate director who is responsible for special areas of work. Since about 3,000 of approximately 33,000 Southern Baptist congregations have full-time music directors—many of these with graduate degress—it is evident that much has been done and that much more will be done.

The state secretary organizes statewide choral festivals, where choirs in the graded choir program are heard by specialists who not only rate them according to accomplishments but give helpful suggestions. There are also statewide schools that meet for a week of instruction, making it possible for church musicians to accumulate credits toward a Church Music diploma.

The publications of the Church Music Department are most extensive, covering just about every aspect of church music activity. For each age-group choir there is a booklet containing helpful suggestions and hints on rehearsal procedures, objectives for the organization, organization of the choral ensemble, lists of recommended selections, and lists of books on choral music, church music, and conducting. A booklet is also available on how to select a church organ.

The Church Music Department is also responsible for publishing graded choir music, instrumental books, solo and ensemble music, hymnals, and songbooks. Its goal is that every congregation should, if possible, have a complete music program of its own. Other publications include *The Junior Musician,* a quarterly for children and young people that contains several selections for treble voice groups, study material in music theory, music puzzles, and a number of articles that disseminate information in an interesting manner and create interest among youth in participating in the church's music program.

The Church Musician, a monthly magazine for adults, is intended not only for choir directors and organists but for choir members, music committee members, pastors, and anyone else interested in church music. The journal contains several compositions for adult choir, accompanied by suggestions for their rehearsal and performance. A number of helpful articles on some phase of church music are to be found in each issue.

c. The National Fellowship of Methodist Musicians

This organization was established 1955 and within ten years had a membership of over 1,000. Its main objective is "to establish and maintain the highest quality of materials and standards of performance in all phases of our ministry," and it has been instrumental in bringing about what improvements have been made in church music over the past ten years.

To carry out its objectives the Fellowship biennially sponsors one-week national conferences, attended by pastors, church musicians, music committee members, choir members, and laymen interested in music. The Fellowship also counsels with colleges and seminaries regarding the selection of curricula and personnel for the training of church musicians. Assistance is given in conducting the type of workshops, institutes, and conferences that will assist their church musicians in attaining the desired objectives on the congregational level.

In alternate years the emphasis is on regional meetings, consisting of church music institutes, held to aid the churches in planning their church music programs and to stimulate them in their thinking, so that the needs of all churches throughout the various conferences may be met. Basic instruction in voice, conducting, organ-playing, music theory, and repertoire are the primary concern at the various district, sub-district, and local church workshops and clinics. Sessions are staffed by the annual conference music committee and/or worship committee, with the Fellowship chapter of the conference cooperating. The church music institutes are planned by a group of leaders from each area, in cooperation with staff members of the General Board of Education.

The Fellowship publishes a monthly periodical, *The Music Ministry,* and numerous pamphlets dealing with various aspects of church music.

The program of the National Fellowship of Methodist Musicians leads to two categories of certification: (1) Minister of Music and (2) Director of Music. The former must be an ordained man and hold a Bachelor's degree with a major in music. The Director of Music may be a lay person. Procedures for certification are established by the General Board of Education of the Methodist Church.

d. The Joint Commission on Church Music in the Protestant Episcopal Church

This is not an organization for church musicians but a body appointed every three years to give direction nationwide to every phase of musical activity in the Protestant Episcopal Church. At each triennial meeting of the church the Joint Commission issues a church music activities report, which includes a specific review of developments and needs in church music.

For the past eighteen years the Joint Commission has sponsored regional summer schools and encouraged parish musicians to associate with the Royal School of Church Music in England, for which there is no parallel organization in the States. It has also published a number of pamphlets on musical subjects—including "music for weddings" and "music for funerals"—and *Music for Nonprofessional Choirs,* a booklet providing objectives and guidelines for the selection of anthems. The Commission was also responsible for publication of *Ideals in Church Music* by Dr. Leo Sowerby.

In 1967 the Commission completed the formulation of a program for accrediting church musicians, patterned after the Archbishop's Diploma course in England. Two examinations are given: one for professional musicians and one for those whose musical activities are avocational. The recently established College of Sacred Music (at the Washington, D. C., cathedral) serves as headquarters for the Commission's work.

e. The Commission on Worship and Church Music of the American Lutheran Church

Like the Episcopal commission, this is not an organization for church musicians. Previous to the merger of 1960 that brought the present American Lutheran Church into being, one of the merging bodies (the Evangelical Lutheran Church) had sponsored a limited

153

program of one-week summer sessions in church music. In 1963 the services of a full-time director of church music were secured, and the program was expanded. In 1964 there were seven one-week church music institutes held, with a total attendance of over 400. Two years later there were nine institutes and 346 attendants. Each of the nineteen districts comprising the present church body has its own committee to implement the program set up by the Commission. In 1965, for example, 68 one-day workshops were held in sixteen districts, with 2,500 attending.

f. The Lutheran Society for Worship, Music, and the Arts

As the title indicates, this organization, founded 1957, has a much broader scope than church music, but music is one of its major concerns, nevertheless. Most of the various Lutheran church bodies are represented in its membership, so that it serves as a kind of coordinating agency that may eventually lead to concerted action on the specific church music problems of American Lutheranism.

One of its accomplishments has been the preparation of a series of texts for use in church music institutes and workshops conducted by its member bodies: the American Lutheran Church, the Lutheran Church of America, and the Lutheran Church—Missouri Synod. During the summer of 1965 these church bodies conducted twenty-four one-week music institutes in twenty states and two Canadian provinces, with a total attendance of about 1,400. The series of prepared texts made it possible to offer a uniform curriculum at all these institutes. Students who successfully completed the prescribed two-year schedule qualified for a certificate in church music.

This coordinated undertaking by the three largest American Lutheran bodies (who comprise 95 percent of all Lutherans in the United States) is an innovation in the right direction. It is hoped that higher achievement certification levels can be set up as the program develops.

The chief publication of the Lutheran Society is *Response,* a quarterly, which because of the broader scope of the Society does not have too many articles that deal specifically with church music.

g. The Fellowship of American Baptist Musicians

This is a recently organized society for musicians belonging to the American Baptist Convention. Recent issues of its newsletter have

154

contained articles on Christian hymnody. It conducts one-week summer sessions in church music, which include classes for church musicians of all categories. Guest speaker at the 1965 session was Dr. Eric Routley, eminent Scotch theologian and author of numerous books on church music.

h. The Commission on Worship of the Lutheran Church in America

Previous to 1965 no churchwide program for the training of church musicians had been conducted by either the Lutheran Church in America or its former components. At the time of the 1963 merger the synods now constituting this body set up a Commission on Worship, which among other things publishes the trimestral *Church Music Memo* as a practical aid to choir directors and organists.

A number of irregularly scheduled summer camps and workshops in church music had been conducted by both the Augustana Church and the United Lutheran Church prior to their 1963 merger. But the first churchwide effort of the LCA was its involvement in the 1965 series of institutes sponsored by the various Lutheran bodies.

i. The Choristers Guild

Founded in 1949, the Guild's activities are not sponsored by a church body but are under the supervision of an independent Board of Directors. Its central purpose is "the development of Christian character through children's choirs."

Members may avail themselves of the various helps which the Guild offers for the organization and development of children's choirs. Its monthly *Letters* contain materials designed to assist in building a well-structured program.

VIII

Coda

It appears that the second half of the twentieth century could very well be the beginning of a glorious period in church music throughout all Protestantism. The one item that could play a major role in realizing this objective is the assistance and sense of direction to be given the work by a dedicated, musically qualified leadership. There can be no leaders if there are no followers. To have both requires organization. Properly directed church music organizations would set the stage for this achievement.

For the most part church musicians here and abroad have been like nomadic tribesmen. They have done the best they could with what they had, but often the potential of the church musician himself was not too superior to that of many in the pews. The imbroglio of Christian music throughout vast areas of today's world is due in large part to desultory if not obtuse practices in the past. It is time the church musician became what he should be: a person *specially* prepared for his work. And it is high time that church leaders of every denomination recognize the need of capable, properly trained musicians in the service of the church. We cannot really expect the church musician to pull himself up by his own bootstraps, and yet any professional preparation our church musicians possess today has been achieved by this kind of do-it-yourself approach.

The following quotation, though written in 1901, is just as applicable today, a good indication of how much real progress (if any) has been made in the past sixty years:

> We can never hope to have a generally adequate conception and appreciation of either the Liturgy or its Music until we have provided for the systematic instruction of both the clergy and the organists in

these departments. Upon the clergyman and the organist, or choirmaster, chiefly rests the great responsibility for a pure and helpful interpretation of the Church's spirit of worship. It is not sufficient for the pastor to know a few historical facts concerning the Liturgy, and for the organist to know the technique of his instrument and have a passing acquaintance with organ and anthem literature.[1]

The church at large has been notoriously unconcerned about the quality of its music. Churchwide departments, boards, and officials are often set up to direct and assist the men's organizations, the women's organizations, the Sunday church school, the youth program, and just about every phase of congregational life. But church musicians and the church music program have by and large been left without assistance and direction.

In gathering information for the concluding pages of this book I sent letters to each of the major Protestant denominations in America, inquiring as to what, if any, church organization had been set up to give assistance in the area of church music. Many a reply was prefaced with "I am sorry to confess . . . I regret to state . . . etc.," indicating that the church group had done very little about the matter but felt nevertheless that there was a real need. Some expressed hopes that some type of organization could be set up in the not-too-distant future.

The only church body that appears to have partly met this need is the Southern Baptist Convention, with the Methodists running a close second. Neither apparently feels that its own church music program is entirely adequate.

It would be unfair, of course, to absolve the individual church musician from *all* responsibility for what has happened. True, his church work is in many instances just a small segment of his total occupational life. True also that his own congregation has not even shown enough interest in his musical advancement to send him to a one-week summer institute, expenses paid. And yet the musician himself has often exhibited a certain complacency and has had no deeply felt need for improvement. The church musician, like anyone else, can lose his sense of perspective, especially if he does not have sufficient contacts with those who could help him raise his sights. It would be well for the organist, if he can do nothing else, to take a Sunday off once in a while and visit some other church that has a good church music program.

---

[1] Harry G. Archer and Luther D. Reed, *The Choral Service Book* (Philadelphia: United Lutheran Publication House, 1901), p. xlii.

Frequently the organist does not sense the importance of his own contribution to worship. Seated at his console, he has the unique opportunity of inviting every person in the church to join solemnly yet joyously in worshiping the Creator of all things. He must not lose sight of the fact that he is *a part of the congregation* and is not there to show off his skill as a performer, to provide background music for subdued conversations, or to entertain.

Obviously it is a little boring to play five or six stanzas of a hymn with exactly the same harmonization and registration, and the aggravation would be multiplied if there were two, three, or more identical services! But a little ingenuity can help ward off some of the triteness and monotony. Granted that few of even the best American organists are capable of improvising their own harmonizations for a given hymn melody—a common practice in Europe.[2] Yet some variety can be injected into the playing of hymns. Every organ has stops labeled flute, oboe, trumpet, etc. Instead of using the trumpet stop, why not use the trumpet itself? The matter of tuning the instrument to the organ could be accomplished to an exact enough degree before the service starts. Supplementing the organ with an instrument or two is obviously to be recommended only in those churches where the performers are not exposed to congregational view.

While the organist is quite in command once the service starts, this does not give him any license to dominate the service. It may not be necessary, for example, to fill up every gap in the service with music.

The composer of church music also has a great responsibility and an almost unlimited opportunity. Since the early sixteenth century, two trends in the composition of church music have converged: (1) the evolution of compositional materials, and (2) the influence of music outside the church. At a time in history when distinctiveness seems taboo and everything is being melted down to an indeterminable blob of gray, people have difficulty seeing that music for the church should be different from any other kind. Only one type of music is really identified almost universally and exclusively with the church and that is the chant. The musical possibilities of the chant may not have been exhausted by church music composers, but perhaps they should also

---

[2] A few years ago I asked a German organist how he liked the chorale book which had been issued some years previously. His reply was to the effect that he thought it was all right, but *why does an organist need a chorale book?* Attending a service in the Moritzkirche in Coburg, Germany, I noticed that an organist in his early twenties—so far as I could determine—played the entire service without a staff of music on his organ rack! His playing can only be described as *tremendous!*

utilize some other styles and idioms which would still distinguish church music from music not meant for use in church. This does not mean, of course, that church music and the composers of church music should drift outside the mainstream of music into some stagnant pool. The main point is that church music needs to be readily identifiable with the church. You just don't expect to hear Gregorian chants or Bach chorales in a ballroom or a corner tavern, and music indigenous to such environs should be just as out of place in church. There needs to be a distinction.

On the other hand we must be wary enough to recognize that not every composition written specifically for the church is going to be appropriate for the occasion. There is probably no other area of music today where one finds such an abundance of meaningless, ostentatious, and vitiated music as among the material purportedly written for church use. The composer who "wears his heart on his sleeve," who feels he has to be different and unique, who tries to impress others by the use of clever devices, who feels he needs to show that he is in command of the most up-to-date harmonic (and *unharmonic!*) devices—such a composer makes no more of a lasting contribution than the one who turns out the most trite or banal or meaningless ditty.

The choir director, too, if he is someone other than the organist, is in a unique position and has unusual responsibilities. His is the opportunity, first of all, to add something to the lives of those with whom he works. He can accept his assignment as a job to be done, the quicker the better, or he can rise to the occasion and imbue his singers with a feeling of growth in Christian living. His general attitude, his incidental comments during rehearsal hours, his demeanor during rehearsals and worship hours will set the tone, consciously or unconsciously, for the behavior of his choir. It takes more than a well-trained, talented musician to spur on such a group to its maximum achievement.

The following, though written by a Roman Catholic, applies fully to the Protestant church musician:

> No matter how great his musical talents otherwise may be, the choir-master who cannot identify his way of thinking with that of the Church, as expressed in her Liturgy, and who fancies that he adequately discharges his duty by merely making *music* whilst a religious function is being gone through, is deficient in one of the most important qualifications for his position.[3]

---

[3] F. X. Haberl, *Magister Choralis* (2nd ed., New York: Frederick Pustet, 1892), p. 225.

The well-schooled, musically sensitive, church-minded choir director will realize that through the choral ensemble each singer is enabled to achieve something greater than he could accomplish alone. This is one of the great rewards of the director's profession.

The most difficult task for most choir directors is the selection of music. This is where a qualified church music organization can make a significant contribution. The following points up this problem:

> In the numerous seasonal brochures received by the writers each year listing choral and organ music, the organ lists reveal an attempt on the part of many organists to perform an extensive cross section of great literature and to keep up with the better new publications. But such is rarely the case with anthems. The choral lists indicate a rut—the same old war horses, chestnuts, and tear-jerkers used year after year, with very few lists indicating that the director has searched out the treasures of past ages or has sorted the wheat from the chaff in the contemporary harvest.[4]

It is easy for the choir director to despair when vocal resources are limited. In such cases it would be well for him to discard the usual meaning attached to the term *choir,* which habitually associates it with part music. The feeling is altogether too prevalent that to be a choir one must sing part music. Granted the desirability of four-part harmony, this should not be a prerequisite for a group that calls itself a choir.

In liturgical services the choir *should* sing the Introit and the Gradual. Scarcely any church would find it impossible to corral a half-dozen youngsters who are musically apt enough to sing *unison* settings of these parts of the liturgy when better-prepared singers are not available. For nonliturgical churches—and these are becoming scarcer as the years pass—there are a number of accompanied unison anthems available.

And then there is the choir member himself! How did the word "volunteer" ever come to be associated with the church choir? It recalls the imagery of a small-town fire department. Now, if every volunteer choir member would take his work as seriously as the volunteer fireman, it wouldn't be so bad, but many a church choir member would not measure up to such a standard. The English writer Sidney S. Campbell suggests that the only "voluntary" thing about belong-

---

[4] Austin C. Lovelace and William C. Rice, *Music and Worship in the Church* (Nashville: Abingdon, 1960), p. 120.

ing to a choir is the initial decision to join it! After that, you have an unavoidable responsibility to discharge.

Each choir member is first of all a worshiper—as indeed are the choir director and the organist. The chorister comes to church primarily to worship. The fact that he sits in a specially assigned area should not detract from this at all. Every time he opens his mouth to utter a sound, he engages in an act of worship. As he participates in choral responses, motets, or anthems, he is bearing up on the wings of his music all the worshipers who have come to the house of God.

Unfortunately, much church architecture belies this concept of the choir's function. The location of the choir often suggests that they are singing *to* the congregation and not *for* it or *with* it. Those parts of the service that the choir sings alone are to be sung on behalf of the congregation just as truly as the pastor offers prayers on their behalf.

When the choir is located where it is openly visible to those in the nave, it detracts from the feeling of worship that both the chorister and the man in the pew should be experiencing. Not only is the choir poorly located in many churches, but one might also question the appropriateness of the choir processional and recessional, a bit of ritual inherited from the days of St. Chrysostom, who back in the fourth century organized singing processionals, with crosses and lighted torches, to parade through the streets after sunset. One could ask whether such parading is really an act of worship. Somehow it seems to militate against thinking of the individual choir member as one of the worshipers.

In these pages the organist and choir director may perhaps have seen intermittent glimpses of themselves as others see them. If a rehearsal of what has happened in the past four hundred years has given any new or enlarged meaning to their work, then the primary objective of this volume has been achieved.

Bibliography

Bibliography

1. ADLER, GUIDO. *Handbuch der Musikgeschichte*. Berlin: Max Hesse, 1930.
2. ALLARD, F. M. *Från Luther till Bach*. Stockholm: Svenska Kyrkans Diakonistyrelses Bokförlag, 1932.
3. ANDERSON, OTTO. *Musikk og Musikkinstrumenter*. Stockholm: Albert Bonnier; Oslo: H. Aschehoug; Copenhagen: J. H. Schultz, 1933.
4. ARCHER, HARRY G., and REED, LUTHER D. *The Choral Service Book*. Philadelphia: United Lutheran Publication House, 1901.
5. ARMSTRONG, THOMAS. "Church Music Today," *Ch. Mus. Soc. Occ. Papers*, No. 17. London: Oxford, 1946.
6. ARNOLD, JOHN. *Church Music Reformed: or the Art of Psalmody*. London: R. Brown, L. Hawes, 1765.
7. ARNOLD, JOHN. *The Complete Psalmodist*. London: G. Bigg, 1779.
8. BACHMANN, D. JOHANNES. *Geschichte des evangelischen Kirchengesanges in Mecklenburg*. Rostock: Stiller, 1881.
9. BALSLEV, C. F. *Den Lutherske Kirkesang i Danmark*. Copenhagen: P. Haase, 1934.
10. BEGG, JAMES. *The Use of Organs and Other Instruments of Music in Christian Worship Indefensible*. Glasgow & London: W. R. M'Phun, 1866.
11. BELL, MAURICE F. *The Arts of the Church: Church Music*. London: A. R. Mowbray, 1909.
12. BENSON, LOUIS E. *The English Hymn, Its Development and Use*. New York: George H. Doran, 1915.
13. BENSON, LOUIS E. *The Hymnody of the Christian Church*. Richmond: John Knox, 1956.
14. BLEW, WILLIAM C. A. *Organs and Organists in Parish Churches*. London: William Reeves, 1878.
15. BLUME, FRIEDRICH. *Die evangelische Kirchenmusik*. Potsdam: Academische Verlagsgesellschaft Athenaion M. B. H., 1931.
16. BONNER, D. F. *Instrumental Music in the Worship of God Divinely Authorized*. Rochester, N. Y.: F. A. Capwell, 1851.
17. BORNEFELD, HELMUT. *Orgelbau und Neue Orgelmusik*. Kassel und Basel: Bärenreiter Verlag, 1952.
18. BRADLEY, CYRIL. "Anthems," *Ch. Mus. Soc. Occ. Papers*, No. 7. London: Humphrey Milford, no date.

19. BRIDGE, SIR FREDERICK. *Samuel Pepys, Lover of Musique.* London: Smith, Elder, 1903.
20. BRITTON, ALLEN P. "The Singing School Movement in the United States," *Report of the Eighth Congress of International Musicological Society,* 1961.
21. BRUINSMA, HENRY A. "The Organ Controversy in the Netherlands Reformation to 1640," *Journal of the American Musicological Society,* VII, 1954.
22. BUCHHOLZ, FRIEDRICH. *Von Bindung und Freiheit der Musik und des Musikers in der Gemeinde.* Kassel: Bärenreiter, 1955.
23. BUKOFZER, MANFRED. *Music in the Baroque Era.* New York: W. W. Norton, 1947.
24. BUKOFZER, MANFRED. *Studies in Medieval and Renaissance Music.* New York: W. W. Norton, 1950.
25. BUMPUS, JOHN S. *History of English Cathedral Music 1549-1889.* London: T. Werner Laurie, 1908.
26. BURNEY, CHARLES. *The Present State of Music in Germany.* London: T. Becket, J. Robson, G. Robinson, 1775.
27. CAMPBELL, SIDNEY S. *Music in the Church.* London: Dennis Dobson, 1951.
28. CANNON, RICHARD L. *Defense of Classic Church Music.* Cincinnati: Methodist Book Concern, 1921.
29. CHASE, GILBERT. *America's Music.* New York: McGraw-Hill, 1955.
30. *Church Music and Musical Life in Pennsylvania in the Eighteenth Century.* Philadelphia: Committee on Historical Research of the Pennsylvania Society of the Colonial Dames of America, 1926.
31. CONWAY, MARMADUKE P. *Organ Voluntaries.* (Ch. Mus. Soc. Occ. Papers No. 18.) London: Oxford, 1948.
32. CORNWALL, N. E. *Music: as It Was, and as It Is.* New York: D. Appleton, 1851.
33. CROSSLEY-HOLLAND, PETER. *Music in Wales.* London: Hinrichsen, 1948.
34. CURWEN, JOHN S. *Studies in Worship Music, First Series.* London: J. Curwen, 1880.
35. CURWEN, JOHN S. *Studies in Worship Music, Second Series.* London: J. Curwen, 1885.
36. DANIEL, R. B. *Chapters on Church Music.* London: Elliot Stock, 1894.
37. DAVID, HANS T. and MENDEL, ARTHUR. *The Bach Reader.* New York: W. W. Norton, 1945.
38. DAVIES, H. WALFORD. "Music and Christian Worship," *Ch. Mus. Soc. Occ. Papers,* No. 4. No date.
39. DAVIES, WALFORD and GRACE, HARVEY. *Music and Worship.* London: Eyre and Spottiswoode, 1935.
40. DAVISON, ARCHIBALD T. *Church Music—Illusion and Reality.* Cambridge: Harvard University Press, 1952.
41. DAVISON, ARCHIBALD T. *Protestant Church Music in America.* Boston: E. C. Schirmer, 1933.
42. DAVISON, ARCHIBALD and APEL, WILLI. *Historical Anthology of Music.* Cambridge: Harvard University, 1950.
43. DICKINSON, EDWARD. *Music in the History of the Western Church.* New York: Scribner's, 1923.

44. DODWELL, HENRY. *A Treatise Concerning the Lawfulness of Instrumental Musick in Holy Offices.* London: William Haws, 1700.
45. DOUGLAS, WINFRED. *Church Music in History and Practice.* New York: Scribner's, 1937.
46. DOUGLAS, WINFRED and ELLINWOOD, LEONARD. *Church Music in History & Practice.* New York: Scribner's, 1962.
47. EHMANN, WILHELM. *Erziehung zur Kirchenmusik.* Gütersloh: Rufer Verlag, 1951.
48. EHMANN, WILHELM. *Kirchenmusik Vermächtnis und Aufgabe.* Darmstadt-Eberstadt: Tonkunst-Verlag, Karl Merseburger, no date.
49. ELLERHORST, WINFRED. *Handbuch der Orgelkunde.* A. G./Einseldeln, Switzerland: Benziger, 1936.
50. ELLINWOOD, LEONARD. "English Influence in American Church Music," *Proceedings of the Royal Musical Association,* 1953.
51. ELLINWOOD, LEONARD. *The History of American Church Music.* New York: Morehouse-Gorham, 1953.
52. ELSON, LOUIS C. *The History of American Music.* New York: Macmillan, 1925.
53. ETHERINGTON, CHARLES L. *The Organist and Choirmaster.* New York: Macmillan, 1952.
54. ETHERINGTON, CHARLES L. *Protestant Worship Music.* New York: Holt, Rinehart, and Winston, 1962.
55. FARMER, HENRY GEORGE. *A History of Music in Scotland.* London: Hinrichsen, 1947.
56. FELLOWES, EDMUND H. *English Cathedral Music, from Edward VI— Edward VII.* London: Methuen, 1941.
57. FELLOWES, E. H. "English Church Music to 1900," *Musical Year Book,* IV-V (1947-48). London: Hinrichsen.
58. FENDT, LEONHARD. *Der lutherische Gottesdienst des 16. Jahrhunderts.* München: Ernst Reinhardt, 1923.
59. FISHER, WILLIAM ARMS. *Notes on Music in Old Boston.* Boston: Oliver Ditson Co., 1918.
60. FOOTE, HENRY WILDER. *Three Centuries of American Hymnody.* Cambridge: Harvard University Press, 1940.
61. "Forty Years of Cathedral Music, 1898-1938" *Ch. Mus. Soc. Occ. Papers,* No. 13. London: Humphrey Milford, 1940.
62. FOSTER, MYLES BIRKET. *Anthems and Anthem Composers.* London: Novello, 1901.
63. FROTSCHER, GOTTHOLD. *Geschichte des Orgelspiels und der Orgelkomposition.* Berlin-Schöneberg: Max Hesse, 1935, 1936.
64. FULLER-MAITLAND, J. A. "The Need for Reform in Church Music," *Ch. Mus. Soc. Occ. Papers,* No. 1. London: Henry Frowde, 1910.
65. GALPIN, FRANCIS W. *Old English Instruments of Music.* London: Methuen, 1910.
66. GARDNER, GEORGE and NICHOLSON, SYDNEY H. *A Manual of English Church Music.* London: SPCK, 1936.
67. GIRARDEAU, JOHN L. *Instrumental Music in the Public Worship of the Church.* Richmond, Va.: Whittet & Shepperson, 1888.
68. GOULD, NATHANIEL DUREN. *Church Music in America.* Boston: A. N. Johnson, 1853.

69. GRACE, HARVEY. *The Complete Organist.* London: Grant Richards, 1920.
70. GRACIE, G. H. HEATH. "Music in the New Cathedrals" *Ch. Mus. Soc. Occ. Papers,* No. 12. London: SPCK, before 1940.
71. GREEN, H. L. A. "The Royal School of Church Music," *Musical Year Book,* Vol. IV-V (1947-48). London: Hinrichsen.
72. HABERL, F. X. *Magister Choralis. A Theoretical and Practical Manual of Gregorian Chant.* Second English Edition. New York: Frederick Pustet, 1892.
73. HADOW, SIR W. H. *Church Music.* London: Longmans, Green, 1926.
74. HAMMERICH, ANGUL. *Dansk Musikhistorie intil ca. 1700.* Copenhagen: G. E. C. Gade, 1921.
75. HARMAN, ALEC and MELLERS, WILFRED. *Man and His Music: the Story of Musical Experience in the West.* New York: Oxford, 1962.
76. HEINISCH, G. FR. *Der Gemeindegesang in der evangelischen Kirche.* Bayreuth: Buchner, 1848.
77. HELLERSTRÖM, A. O. T. *Liturgik.* Stockholm: Svenska Kyrkans Diakonistyrelses Bokförlag, 1940.
78. HEROLD, MAX. *Alt-Nürnberg in seinen Gottesdiensten.* Gütersloh: C. Bertelsmann, 1890.
79. HEYDT, JOHANN DANIEL V. D. *Geschichte der evangelischen Kirchenmusik.* Berlin: Trowitzsch, 1926.
80. HINRICHSEN, MAX. *Organ and Choral Aspects and Prospects.* London: Bach House, 1958.
81. HINRICHSEN, MAX. *Musical Year Book,* Vols. IV-V. London: Hinrichsen, 1947-48.
82. HOOD, GEORGE. *A History of Music in New England.* Boston: Wilkins, Carter, 1846.
83. HOWARD, JOHN TASKER. *Our American Music.* New York: Thomas Y. Crowell, 1939.
84. HOWARD, JOHN TASKER. *Our American Music.* New York: Thomas Y. Crowell, 1946.
85. HOWE, GRANVILLE L. *A Hundred Years of Music in America.* Chicago: G. L. Howe, 1889.
86. HUBBARD, W. L. *History of American Music.* Toledo: Irving Squire, 1908.
87. HUNT, JOSEPH M. *Music in the Church.* Kansas City, Mo.: J. M. Hunt, 1900.
88. HUNTER, S. A. *Music and Religion.* New York: Abingdon, 1930.
89. INGRAM, MADELINE D. *Organizing and Directing Children's Choirs.* New York: Abingdon, 1959.
90. JAKOB, GEORG. *Die Kunst im Dienste der Kirche.* Landshut: Jos. Thomann, 1870.
91. JEBB, JOHN. *The Choral Responses and Litanies of the United Church of England and Ireland.* London: George Bell, 1847.
92. KAPPNER, GERHARD. *Sakrament und Musik.* Gütersloh: C. Bertelsmann, 1952.
93. KENNARD, FRANCIS T. *The Organization and Training of Parish Choirs.* London: Proprietors of *Musical Opinion,* 1920.
94. KETTRING, DONALD. *Steps Toward a Singing Church.* Philadelphia: Westminster, 1948.

95. KINKELDEY, OTTO. *Orgel und Klavier in der Musik des 16. Jahrhunderts.* Leipzig: Breitkopf & Härtel, 1910.
96. KLOTZ, HANS. *Das Buch von der Orgel.* Kassel: Bärenreiter, 1955.
97. KLOTZ, HANS. *Über die Orgelkunst der Gotik, der Renaissance und des Barock.* Kassel: Bärenreiter, 1934.
98. KOCH, EDUARD EMIL. *Geschichte des Kirchenlieds und Kirchengesangs.* Stuttgart: Chr. Belser, 1866.
99. KOESTLIN, HEINRICH ADOLF. *Geschichte des Christlichen Gottesdienstes.* Freiburg: J. C. B. Mohr, 1887.
100. KOLSRUD, OLUF. Article in *Norvegia Sacra.* Oslo: Steenske Forlag, 1935.
101. KÖSTLIN, HEINRICH ADOLF. *Luther als der Vater des evangelischen Kirchengesanges.* Leipzig: Paul graf Waldersee, 1879-98.
102. KRUTSCHEK, PAUL. *Die Kirchenmusik nach dem Willen der Kirche.* Third edition. New York: F. Pustet, 1891.
103. LANG, PAUL HENRY. *Music in Western Civilization.* New York: W. W. Norton, 1941.
104. LA TROBE, JOHN ANTES. *The Music of the Church.* London: L. B. Seeley, 1831.
105. LAUB, THOMAS. *Musik og Kirke.* Copenhagen: Nordisk Forlag, 1920.
106. LE HURAY, PETER. "The English Anthem 1580-1640," *Proceedings of the Royal Musical Association.* London, 1959-60.
107. LIGHTWOOD, JAMES T. *Methodist Music in the Eighteenth Century.* London: Epworth, 1927.
108. LILIENCRON, R. FREIHERR VON. *Chorordnung für die Sonn- und Festtage des Kirchenjahres.* Gütersloh: C. Bertelsmann, 1900.
109. LILIENCRON, R. FREIHERR VON. *Liturgisch-musikalische Geschichte der evangelischen Gottesdienste von 1523 bis 1700.* Schleswig: Julius Bergas, 1893.
110. LILIENCRON, R. FREIHERR VON. *Ueber den Chorgesang in der evangelischen Kirche.* Berlin: Carl Habel, 1880.
111. LOVE, JAMES. *Scottish Church Music, Its Composers and Sources.* Edinburgh and London: William Blackwood, 1891.
112. LOVELACE, AUSTIN C. *The Organist and Hymn Playing.* Nashville: Abingdon, 1962.
113. LOVELACE, AUSTIN C. and RICE, WILLIAM C. *Music and Worship in the Church.* Nashville: Abingdon, 1960.
114. LOVETT, SYDNEY H. "The Use of Small Church Organs," *Ch. Mus. Soc. Occ. Papers,* No. 20. London: Oxford, no date.
115. LUTKIN, PETER CHRISTIAN. *Music in the Church.* Milwaukee: Young Churchman, 1910.
116. LYON, JAMES. *The Lawfulness, Excellency, and Advantage of Instrumental Music in the Public Worship of God.* Philadelphia: William Dunlap, 1763.
117. MCMILLAN, WILLIAM. *The Worship of the Scottish Reformed Church 1550-1638.* London: James Clarke, 1931.
118. MACDERMOTT, CANON K. H. *The Old Church Gallery Minstrels.* London: SPCK, 1948.
119. MACMILLAN, ERNEST. *Music in Canada.* Toronto: Canadian Music Council, 1955.

120. MANKELL, ABRAHAM. *Musikens Historia.* Örebro: N. M. Lindh, 1864.
121. *Manual of Church Praise According to the Use of the Church of Scotland.* Edinburgh: Church of Scotland Committee on Publications, 1932.
122. *Manual of Presbyterian Law for Church Officers and Members.* Presbyterian Church in the United States of America, 1950.
123. MEES, ARTHUR. *Choirs & Choral Music.* London: John Murray, 1901.
124. MERSMANN, HANS. *Musikgeschichte.* Frankfurt/Main: Hans F. Menck, 1955.
125. METCALF, FRANK J. *American Writers and Compilers of Sacred Music.* New York: Abingdon, 1925.
126. MILLER, PAUL JEROME. *Youth Choirs.* New York: Harold Flammer, 1953.
127. MINSHALL, E. *Fifty Years' Reminiscences of a Free Church Musician.* London: James Clarke, 1910.
128. MOBERG, CARL ALLAN. *Kyrkomusikens Historia.* Stockholm: Svenska Kyrkans Diakonistyrelses Bokförlag, 1932.
129. MOSER, HANS JOACHIM. *Die evangelische Kirchenmusik in Deutschland.* Berlin-Darmstadt: Carl Merseburger, 1954.
130. MOSER, HANS JOACHIM. *Frühmeister der deutschen Orgelkunst.* Wiesbaden: Breitkopf & Härtel, 1930.
131. MOSER, HANS JOACHIM. *Geschichte der deutschen Musik.* Stuttgart und Berlin: J. G. Cotta, 1922.
132. *Music in Church. Report of the Archbishops' Committee.* Westminster: Church Information Board, 1951, revised 1957.
133. *Music in Worship. Report of the Archbishops' Committee.* London: Central Board of Finance of the Church of England, 1922.
134. MÜLLER, KARL and BLANKENBURG, WALTER. *Leiturgia,* Vol. IV. Kassel: Johannes Stauda, 1961.
135. NELLE, WILHELM. *Geschichte des deutschen evangelischen Kirchenliedes.* Leipzig and Hamburg: Gustav Schloessmann, 1928.
136. NETTL, PAUL. *Luther and Music.* Philadelphia: Muhlenberg, 1948.
137. NICHOLSON, SYDNEY H. *Church Music, a Practical Handbook.* London: Faith Press. Third edition, no date.
138. NICHOLSON, SYDNEY H. *Quires and Places Where They Sing.* London: SPCK, 1932.
139. NICHOLSON, SIDNEY H. "The Organ Voluntary," *Ch. Mus. Soc. Occ. Papers,* No. 6. London: Humphrey Milford, no date.
140. NININGER, RUTH. *Church Music Comes of Age.* New York: Carl Fischer, 1957.
141. NODERMANN, PREBEN. *Studier i Svensk Hymnologi.* Lund: Sydsvenska Bok- och Musikförlaget, 1911.
142. NORLIND, TOBIAS. *Svensk Musikhistoria.* Stockholm: Wahlström & Widstrand, 1918.
143. *Of the Use and Abuse of Music* (by a Friend of Church Music). No publisher given. English, 1753.
144. PARRY, W. H. *Thirteen Centuries of English Church Music.* London: Hinrichsen, 1946.
145. PATRICK, MILLAR. *Four Centuries of Scottish Psalmody.* London: Oxford, 1949.
146. PATRICK, MILLAR. *The Story of the Church's Song.* Richmond: John Knox, 1962.

147. PHILLIPS, C. HENRY. *The Singing Church*. London: Faber and Faber, 1943.
148. PIERIK, MARIE. *The Song of the Church*. London: Longmans, Green, 1947.
149. PLAYFORD, JOHN. *A Brief Introduction to the Skill of Musick*. Third Edition. London: W. Godbid, 1660.
150. PRATT, WALDO SELDEN. *The Music of the French Psalter of 1562*. New York: Columbia, 1939.
151. PRATT, WALDO SELDEN. *The Music of the Pilgrims*. Boston: Oliver Ditson, 1921.
152. PRATT, WALDO SELDEN. *Musical Ministries in the Church*. New York: Fleming H. Revell, 1901.
153. PROCTOR, FRANCIS and FRERE, WALTER H. *A New History of the Book of Common Prayer*. London: Macmillan, 1951.
154. REED, LUTHER D. *The Lutheran Liturgy*. Philadelphia: Muhlenberg, 1959. Second Edition.
155. REESE, GUSTAVE. *Music in the Middle Ages*. London: J. M. Dent, 1941.
156. RICE, WILLIAM C. *A Concise History of Church Music*. Nashville: Abingdon, 1964.
157. RICHARDSON, A. MADELEY. *Church Music*. London: Longmans, Green, 1910.
158. RIETSCHEL, D. GEORG. *Die Aufgabe der Orgel im Gottesdienste bis ins 18. Jahrh.* Leipzig: Alexander Edelmann, 1892.
159. RIETSCHEL, GEORG, and GRAFF, PAUL. *Lehrbuch der Liturgik*. Göttingen: Vandenhoeck & Ruprecht, 1951.
160. RIGGENBACH, CHR. JOH. *Kirchengesang in Basel seit der Reformation*. No publ. or date.
161. RIMBAULT, EDWARD F. *The Book of Common Prayer with Musical Notes*. Compiled by John Marbeck. London: J. A. Novello, 1845.
162. RITCHIE and PORTEOUS. *The Organ Question*. London: Groombridge & J. Nisbet, 1856.
163. ROOTHAM, CYRIL BRADLEY. "Anthems," *Ch. Mus. Soc. Occ. Papers*, No. 7. London: Humphrey Milford.
164. ROUTLEY, ERIK. *Church Music and Theology*. Philadelphia: Muhlenberg, 1959.
165. ROUTLEY, ERIK. *The Church and Music*. London: Gerald Duckworth, 1950.
166. ROUTLEY, ERIK R. "The Reformed Churches," *Musical Year Book*, Vols. IV-V. London: Hinrichsen, 1947-48.
167. ROUTLEY, ERIK. *The Organist's Guide to Congregational Praise*. London: Independent Press, 1957.
168. ROUTLEY, ERIK. *Music, Sacred and Profane*. London: Independent Press, 1960.
169. ROUTLEY, ERIK. *The Music of Christian Hymnody*. London: Independent Press, 1957.
170. SACHS, CURT. *Our Musical Heritage*. New York: Prentice-Hall, 1948.
171. SACHSE, JULIUS FRIEDRICH. *Music of the Ephrata Cloister*. Lancaster: by the author, 1903.
172. SANDVIK, O. M. *Norsk Koralhistorie*. Oslo: H. Aschehoug, 1930.
173. SANDVIK, O. M. and SCHJELDERUP, GEHR. *Norges Musikhistorie*. Kristiania: Eberh. B. Oppi-Kunstforlag, 1921.
174. SAUNDERS, PERCY G. *Choir Training*. Croydon, Surrey: Royal School of Church Music, no date.

175. SCHERING, ARNOLD. *Johann Sebastian Bachs Leipziger Kirchenmusik.* Leipzig: VEB Breitkopf & Härtel, 1954.
176. SCHLECHT, RAYMUND. *Geschichte der Kirchenmusik.* Regensburg: Alfred Coppenrath, 1871.
177. SCHLICK, ARNOLD. *Spiegel der Orgelmacher und Organisten.* Mainz: Paul Smets, 1932.
178. SCHOEBERLEIN, LUDWIG. *Die Musik im Cultus der evangelischen Kirche.* Heidelberg: Carl Winter, 1881.
179. SCHOEBERLEIN, LUDWIG. *Schatz des liturgischen Chor- und Gemeindegesangs.* Göttingen: Vandenhoeck & Ruprecht, 1865.
180. SCHOLES, PERCY A. *Dr. Burney's Musical Tours in Europe.* London: Oxford, 1959.
181. SCHOLES, PERCY A. *Oxford Companion to Music.* London: Oxford, 1950.
182. SCHOLES, PERCY A. *The Puritans and Music.* London: Oxford, 1934.
183. SCHWEITZER, ALBERT. *J. S. Bach.* Trans. Ernest Newmann. New York: Macmillan, 1923.
184. SELDEN-GOTH, G. *Felix Mendelssohn Letters.* New York: Pantheon Books, 1945.
185. SHUTTLEWORTH, H. C. *The Place of Music in Public Worship.* London: Elliot Stock, 1892.
186. SIGL, MAX. *Kirchenmusik in ihren Grundfragen.* Regensburg: Josef Kösel & Friedrich Pustet, 1922.
187. SIMS, W. HINES. *Instrumental Music in the Church.* Nashville: Sunday School Board of the Southern Baptist Convention, 1947.
188. SMITH, FLORENCE. *Protestant Church Music.* Butler: Higley Press, 1949.
189. SPITTA, JOHANN AUGUST. *Johann Sebastian Bach.* New York: Dover, 1951.
190. STAHL, WILHELM. *Geschichtliche Entwicklung der evangelischen Kirchenmusik.* Berlin: Max Hesse, 1920.
191. STAPLES, H. J. *The Choirmaster and Organist.* London: Epworth, 1939.
192. STATHAM, HEATHCOTE. "Restoration Church Music," *Ch. Mus. Soc. Occ. Papers,* No. 19. London: Oxford, 1949.
193. STEVENS, DENIS. *Tudor Church Music.* London: Faber and Faber, 1961.
194. STEWART, G. W. *Music in the Church.* London: A. & C. Black, 1914.
195. STEWART, G. W. *Music in Church Worship.* London: Hodder and Stoughton, 1926.
196. STEVENSON, ROBERT M. *Patterns of Protestant Church Music.* Durham: Duke University Press, 1953.
197. STORM, FREDRICK. *Traek af den religiöse Musiks og Orglets Historie.* Trondheim: T. A. Höeg, 1845.
198. SUMNER, WILLIAM LESLIE. *The Organ.* New York: Philosophical Library, 1952.
199. SÖRENSEN, SÖREN. *Kirkens Liturgi.* Copenhagen: Munkegaard, 1952.
200. "The Choral Foundations in the Church of England," *Ch. Mus. Soc. Occ. Papers,* No. 8. London: Humphrey Milford.
201. "The Present State of Cathedral Music," *Ch. Mus. Soc. Occ. Papers,* No. 11. London: Humphrey Milford.
202. THUNER, O. E. *Dansk Salme-Leksikon.* Copenhagen: O. Lohse, 1930.
203. TOOP, AUGUSTUS. *The Organist and His Choir.* London: Musical Opinion, 1925.
204. TOWNSEND, W. J., WORKMAN, H. B., and EAYRS, GEORGE. *A New History of Methodism.* London: Hodder and Stoughton, 1909.

205. VINCENT, WILLIAM. *Considerations on Parochial Music.* London: T. Cadell, 1787.
206. VOSSELLER, ELIZABETH VAN FLEET. *The Use of a Children's Choir in Church.* New York: H. W. Gray, 1907.
207. WACKERNAGEL, CARL E. P. *Das Deutsche Kirchenlied.* Stuttgart: S. G. Lieschire, 1841.
208. WALKER, ERNEST. *A History of Music in England.* Oxford: Clarendon, 1952.
209. WEINMANN, KARL. *History of Church Music.* New York: Fr. Pustet, 1910.
210. WESLEY, SAMUEL SEBASTIAN. *A Few Words on Cathedral Music and the Musical System of the Church.* London: F. & J. Rivington, 1849.
211. WESTBROOK, FRANCIS B. "A Short History of Methodist Music," *Musical Year Book,* Vols. IV-V. London: Hinrichsen, 1947-48.
212. WHITLEY, W. T. *Congregational Hymn Singing.* London: J. M. Dent, 1933.
213. WILLIAMS, C. LEE, and BREWER, A. HERBERT. *Church Music: a Plea for a Simple Service in Village, Town and Cathedral.* Gloucester: Chance & Bland, no date.
214. WINTERFELD, CARL VON. *Der evangelische Kirchengesang.* Leipzig: Breitkopf und Härtel, 1943.
215. WOLFRUM, PHILIPP. *Die Entstehung und erste Entwickelung des deutschen evang. Kirchenliedes.* Leipzig: Breitkopf & Härtel, 1890.
216. YOUNG, PERCY M. *The Choral Tradition.* London: Hutchinson, 1962.
217. ZELLE, FRIEDRICH. *Das erste evangelische Choralbuch.* Berlin: Weidmann, 1903.

Index

Index

Index

Musica Getutscht, 8
Music, The A.G.O. Magazine, 150

National Fellowship of Methodist Musicians, 152, 153
New Bach Society, 80
Newte, F., 58
Norges Kirkensangforbund, 136
Notation of music, early, 1, 9

Obrecht, Jakob, 35
Okeghem, Johannes, 24, 66
Opera, Biblical, 68
Opera, influence on church music, 34, 67, 68, 95
Oratorios, early performances of, 36, 47, 82
Organ accompanying congregational singing, 15, 17, 18, 19, 38, 39, 43-45, 48, 52, 74, 87
Organ, added in the service, 2; American, 104-05, 128-29; baroque, 6; early in America, 110-13; early manufacturing of, 4; early use in Brazil, 145; in Denmark, 7, 21, 22, 50, 82; in England, 7, 26, 32, 57, 89, 90, 91, 104, 105, 106; in Germany, 3, 6, 14, 16; in Iceland, 99, 134; in Finland, 83; in the Netherlands, 25, 64, 65, 85; in Norway, 7, 21, 22, 50, 82, 96; in Scotland, 26, 84, 85, 86, 87, 99, 100, 101, 102, 105; in Sweden, 7, 21, 22, 48, 83; in Switzerland, 23, 24, 51, 84; in the United States, 110, 111, 112, 118
early use in worship, 1-4, 22
excluded by Protestants, 3, 4, 21, 23, 24, 25, 26, 32, 45, 52, 54, 55, 91, 100, 101, 104, 106, 119
"gadgets," 45, 81
literature, early, 7, 8, 39
renaissance, 6
Organists playing secular music, 16, 17, 83, 95, 98, 118
Organs destroyed under Puritans, 54; reinstated under the Restoration, 55, 57, 90
Organs (large, portative, positive), 4, 5, 6, 7
Osiander, Lukas, 18, 38, 40, 41, 121

Ousley, Frederick, 108
Oxford Movement, in England, 106, 127; in the United States, 121, 122, 127

Pachelbel, Johann, 35, 42
"Pair of organs," 105
Palestrina, 10, 30, 34, 67, 73
Parochial Service, 29
Parry, Hubert, 126
Passion, 35, 36, 47, 68, 69, 77, 80, 82
Paumann, Conrad, 8
Pedals, introduced, 6; at time of J. S. Bach, 71, 72; early use in England, 7, 57, 90, 99, 104, 105
Pepys, Samuel, 63
Peri, Giacopo, 34
Peter, Johann, 117
Pietism, effect on church music, 47, 49, 68, 78, 93, 94, 95
Playford, John, 62
Porteous, Dr., 101
Praetorius, Michael, 37, 38, 49
Pratt, Waldo Selden, 147
Praxis pietatis melica, 48
Prayer Book, see Book of Common Prayer
Precentor, 49, 52, 53, 86, 99, 103, 115
Printing of music, early, 9
Purcell, Henry, 31, 32, 63, 103, 146
Puritans and church music, 26, 27, 32, 33, 53-55, 56, 57, 62, 88, 106, 112

Quartet, introduced in England, 108; in the United States, 122, 123, 125; in Canada, 146

Rationalism, effect on church music, 83, 93, 95, 96
Regal, 5
Reger, Max, 95
Reinken, Jan, 69, 72, 91
Response, 154
Rheinberger, Joseph, 96
Richards, Emerson, 148
Rietschel, D. Georg, 43-45
Ritchie, Dr., 101
Routley, Eric, 33, 108, 155
Royal Canadian College of Organists, 147, 150
Royal College of Organists, 130, 147

Type, 11 on 13 and 10 on 11 Times Roman
Display, Optima, Folio, Times Roman
Paper, R Antique